Edinburgh New Trams

GAVIN BOOTH

Key Books

TRANSPORT SYSTEMS SERIES, VOLUME 14

Front cover image: Tram 272 sweeps round from North St Andrew Street into York Place in June 2014 on the last leg of its journey to the original York Place terminus. Beyond it, Edinburgh stretches north towards the Firth of Forth and the hills of Fife.

Title page image: With Edinburgh's Old Town in the background, one of Edinburgh's 27 CAF Urbos 100 trams climbs towards the St Andrew Square stop on the last lap of its journey to York Place in February 2017.

Contents page image: Tram 268 on the grassed reservation by Edinburgh Park in March 2023, carrying advertising for the open-top tours offered by its sister company, Lothian Buses.

Back cover image: Trams 276 and 258 meet at the Port of Leith tram stop in January 2024.

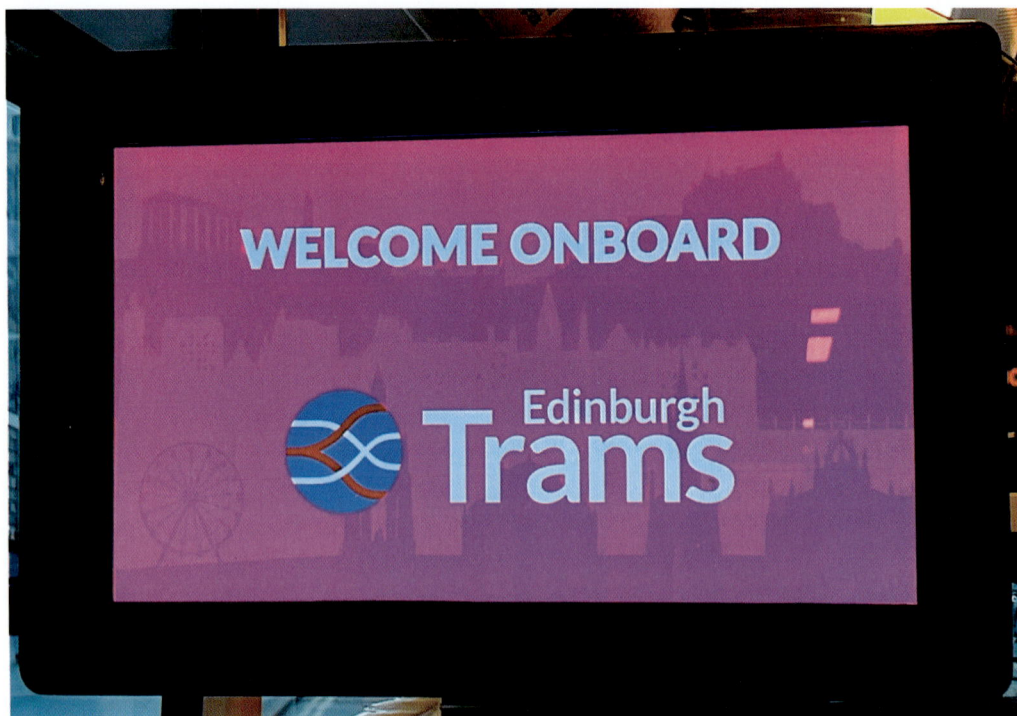

Published by Key Books
An imprint of Key Publishing Ltd
PO Box 100
Stamford
Lincs PE9 1XQ

www.keypublishing.com

The right of Gavin Booth to be identified as the author of this book has been asserted in accordance with the Copyright, Designs and Patents Act 1988 Sections 77 and 78.

Copyright © Gavin Booth, 2025

ISBN 978 1 80282 035 7

Typeset by SJmagic DESIGN SERVICES, India.

Contents

Preface   4

Introduction   7

Chapter 1   Early Initiatives   13

Chapter 2   A Difficult Birth   20

Chapter 3   Hold the Front Page!   38

Chapter 4   The Trams   44

Chapter 5   To York Place, Newhaven – and Beyond   52

Chapter 6   Enjoy the Journey   58

Preface

When growing up in Edinburgh in the 1940s and 1950s, the city's trams were a part of everyday life, taking me to school, 'up town' to the city centre, and to visit grandparents. After what turned out to be an ill-judged 30-year flirtation with cable cars, chosen because of the city's many hills, Edinburgh Corporation proceeded to electrify the whole system in the early 1920s, investing in new trams and upgrading former cable cars, eventually growing to a 28-route system covering 76.04km (47¼ route miles) with a tram fleet that hovered around the 360 mark for 20 years. The relative youth of the fleet – the newest trams were built by the corporation in 1950 – meant that it could have lasted longer than it did, but from 1952 a programme designed to replace all the tram routes in favour of buses meant that the number left in the fleet dropped until there were just 99 cars left at the start of 1956. On 16 November that year, the city's last first-generation tram rolled into the depot and few would have imagined that 58 years later trams would once again carry passengers along Edinburgh's streets.

Although I spent my career in and around the bus industry, I have always had an affection for trams. My family used to feign surprise when they realised that there was a tramway system in most of the places we went on

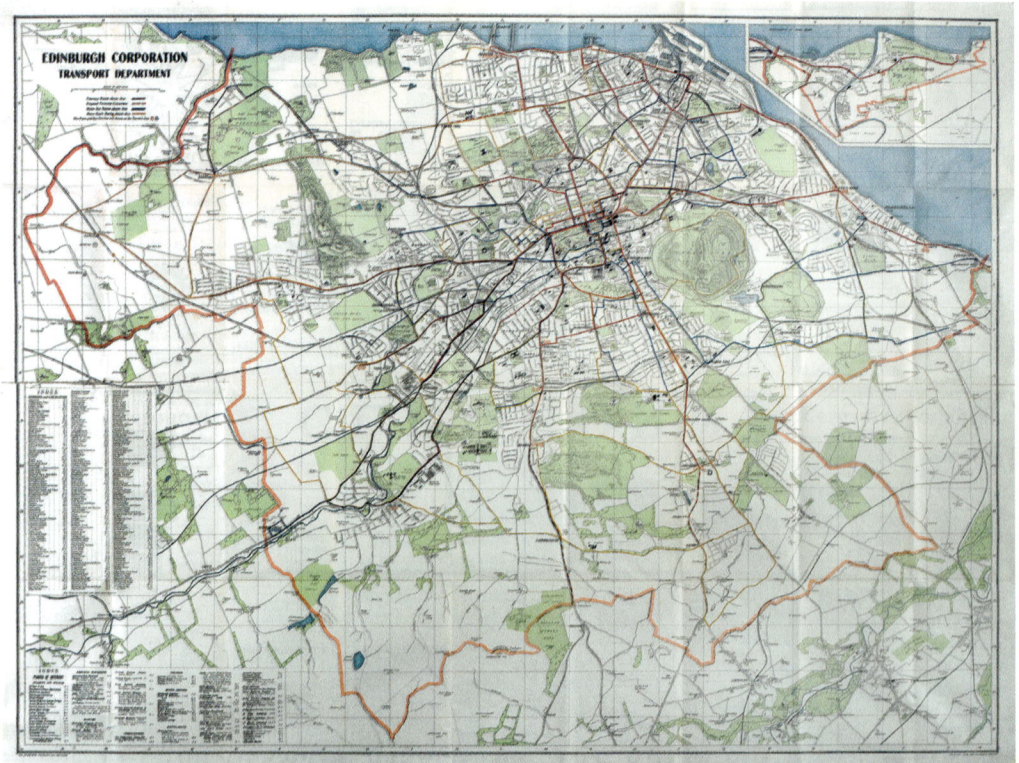

A 1936 Edinburgh Corporation map reveals almost the full extent of the city's original electric tramways – tram routes are shown in red. The system was extended south to Fairmilehead in 1935 and west to Corstorphine in 1937, but planned extensions south to Hillend and Kaimes were never built.

RIGHT: Princes Street witnessed a constant procession of Edinburgh's previous-generation trams. This early 1950s view from the Scott Monument shows the east end of the street with 20 trams in view. The 21st-century trams follow the route of the tram in the foreground, emerging from South St Andrew Street on the left and proceed westwards.

BELOW: On 16 November 1956, Edinburgh's last tram was driven through the gates of Shrubhill works, and while many among the crowds might have wished trams would return to the city streets, few believed it would happen decades later.

If construction of the new Edinburgh trams had started later, there may have been no need for overhead wiring in streets including Princes Street and the trams could have glided along under battery power just as they do in Nice, France, Edinburgh's twin town. This five-section 35m-long (114.83ft) Alstom Citadis in Nice uses on-board nickel metal hydride batteries without its pantograph in October 2008.

holiday. Firstly Blackpool, inevitably, but then our horizons widened and my children were not surprised to discover trams on many holidays overseas – to Belgium, Italy, the Netherlands, Spain and particularly Portugal. And since then, I have been fortunate to explore the tramway systems in cities such as Budapest, Prague and Vienna, and in countries including France, Germany, Sweden, Switzerland and the United States.

So, I was excited when a new tramway was proposed for Edinburgh, but, as we shall see, this nearly did not happen, such was the opposition from many citizens and politicians, and there were concerns over the ever-rising cost of the project. The tramway eventually opened in 2014, late, over-budget and truncated, and despite everything, it has since grown and its future is looking bright.

You may detect that I am very pro-tram, but it would be wrong to paint a cosy picture of the planning and construction process of the new Edinburgh trams, ignoring the controversies and widespread opposition that nearly led to the abandonment of the scheme at various times. I would never pretend that it was all plain sailing, but lessons appear to have been learned and the second phase of Line 1 was built and is carrying passengers in a considerably shorter timescale than the first phase and with much less hassle and inconvenience to Edinburgh's citizens and the many visitors to the city.

The uncredited photographs in this book are mine or from my collection; Keith McGillivray has helpfully plugged some gaps and these are credited to him.

Gavin Booth
Edinburgh

Tramway construction was very labour-intensive, and arguably quicker, in the 1900s. Track-laying work is seen in progress at the Foot of Leith Walk; this is a section of route covered since 2023 by the extension of the new Edinburgh Trams to Newhaven.

Introduction

In November 1956, huge crowds watched Edinburgh's last electric tram make its final journey, defeated by the all-conquering motor bus. Once there had been roundly 200 tramway systems throughout the United Kingdom, operated by horse trams, petrol trams, gas trams, cable trams, and mainly electric trams, but with the closure of the Edinburgh system, there were just six left – in Aberdeen, Blackpool, Glasgow, Leeds, Liverpool and Sheffield – and by the end of 1962, only the Blackpool coastal tramway survived.

In some parts of continental Europe, the situation was very different, with thriving tramway systems that benefited from route extensions as well as investment in new tramcars that were very different to the double-deckers once so familiar in the UK. Continental systems were buying single-deckers that became longer and more sophisticated as the decades passed.

Over a century ago, there were tramway systems of all sizes in the UK, municipally owned, company owned and even privately owned. At first, they were a source of local pride, a sign of urban sophistication and by the mid-1920s, there were some 14,000 trams in use throughout Britain. By the mid-1930s, however, many of these systems had closed, often because the cost of replacing elderly trams and maintaining the track had become prohibitive. Another factor that hastened the end of the UK's first-generation systems was their status as street tramways. Ultimately, the growth in private motoring squeezed the trams out of existence. In the 1930s, many tramways had been replaced by trolleybuses, taking advantage of municipal electricity, and in turn these were being replaced by motor buses.

This is no.35, one of Edinburgh's first-generation trams, built by Edinburgh Corporation at Shrubhill in 1948 and now in preservation at the Crich Tramway Village in Derbyshire. In 1988, it was one of five trams (one Edinburgh, one Blackpool, one Paisley and two Glasgow) carrying passengers around the Glasgow Garden Festival.

LEFT: A memory of Edinburgh's cable cars survives in the road at the western end of Waterloo Place, leading into Princes Street. It had survived to the end of the tramway to this point in 1954, and was subsequently relocated to the centre of the road.

BELOW: The 21st-century Edinburgh trams were numbered 251–277, unused numbers in the Lothian Buses fleet. There were first-generation electric trams with these numbers in the Edinburgh Corporation fleet – this is the original 258, a 1932 Pickering-built car, at the Foot of Leith Walk in the early 1950s, an area now served by the new 258 on journeys between Newhaven and Edinburgh Airport.

The new tram 258 in Constitution Street, on test, in May 2023.

The Edinburgh Corporation tramway system reached its peak in 1937, operating on high frequencies by a hard-working fleet of 360 double-deck trams. By 1956, it seemed impossible that trams would ever serve the population of Edinburgh again, and, in truth, even when a new tramway was built more than 50 years later, there were times when it seemed that electric trams would never be seen on the city's streets again.

During the 1970s, there was a renewed interest in light rail as an alternative to diesel buses. In response, two new systems opened in the 1980s – the Tyne & Wear Metro in 1980 and the Docklands Light Railway in London in 1987. Although these were off-street light metro systems running on segregated track, rather than

Britain's first electric tramway opened in Blackpool in 1885 and, with only a short break for upgrading in 2011–12, has operated continuously. Between 2011 and 2017, it bought 32.2m- (105.64ft)-long, five-section Bombardier Flexity Swifts; no.012 is seen in July 2013.

Greater Manchester Metrolink was the first of the modern systems when it opened in 1992 and is now the most extensive tramway in Britain. Flexity Swifts like these replaced the original trams between 2009 and 2022. The 28.4m (93.18ft)-long trams, which regularly work in pairs, are not low-floor like those used by other new-generation British systems. These examples are seen in March 2016.

tramways, they helped encourage fresh interest in urban light rail. The Blackpool tramway, running more or less continuously since 1885, was joined by the UK's first new generation tramway in 1992, the Greater Manchester Metrolink. Between 1994 and 2004, four new tramways opened – South Yorkshire Supertram in 1994, West Midlands Metro in 1999, Croydon Tramlink (now London Trams) in 2000 and Nottingham Express Transit in 2004. Meanwhile the Blackpool tramway had been upgraded as a modern light rail system and reopened in 2012. An extension into the town centre started operating in 2024.

The Manchester system has grown spectacularly, and now operates over a 100.58km (62½)-mile network, with plans for further expansion. In mileage terms, the South Yorkshire system is 35.4km (22 miles), Nottingham

ABOVE: South Yorkshire Supertram first opened in 1994–95 with a fleet of 34.75m (114ft)-long three-section Siemens trams, as seen here in September 2017, when the system was run by Stagecoach. The first tram-trains in Britain are also operated in South Yorkshire.

RIGHT: The Midland Metro, now the West Midlands Metro, opened between Birmingham and Wolverhampton in 1999 and has been subsequently extended. The fleet consists of 32.96m (108.14ft)-long five-section CAF Urbos trams, as here. This tram is leaving the Grand Central (New Street Station) stop in central Birmingham in September 2016.

Nottingham Express Transit first opened in 2004 with a fleet of five-section, 33m (108ft)-long Bombardier Incentro trams, as seen in September 2007.

Croydon Tramlink, now London Trams, opened in 2000, using 30.1m (98.75ft)-long Bombardier Flexity Swifts, joined in 2011–16 by 32.4m (106.3ft)-long five-section Stadler Variobahn trams, as shown here in September 2017.

32.19km (20 miles), London 28.16km (17½ miles), West Midlands 24.14km (15 miles), Blackpool 19.31km (12 miles) and the newest, Edinburgh, 18.5km (11½ miles). The Blackpool tramway has extended inland, and West Midlands continues to spread outwards.

So, while trams have made a welcome return to British streets, our near neighbours in France have really embraced the tram for their towns and cities, introducing some 30 new systems since 1985.

After a difficult start, Edinburgh's trams are well established in the city and there are ambitious plans for expansion. This is the story of how, after much acrimonious discussion and serious threats to abandon the whole project, the tramway was eventually built and opened, and subsequently successfully extended to cover a major portion of the originally planned route.

Chapter 1

Early Initiatives

The first stirrings of a renewed enthusiasm for trams returning to the streets of Edinburgh came in the late 1980s when Lothian Regional Council showed an interest in developing two Metro lines. The preferred strategy foresaw an east–west line starting in Leith, then through the city centre and west by Haymarket, with a branch north towards Granton, then by Gorgie to terminate at the 1970s major housing development at Wester Hailes. There was an ambitious north–south line too, starting at termini in the north-west of the city and heading south with possible extensions beyond the Edinburgh boundary into Midlothian. What made this ambitious was the prospect of a long section through the city centre that would be underground. Both of these lines would be served by a depot in Leith. Plans for the north–south line were abandoned in 1993 due to increasing costs. As we shall see, the new Edinburgh tramway that opened for business more than 20 years later covers major sections of the suggested east–west route and a north–south line is still on the wish-list, though purely as a surface tramway.

There were private sector plans put forward by the Edinburgh Tram Company in 1996 for a line linking Haymarket, just west of the city centre, through the centre and north to Leith, using lightweight Roadliner trams on low-profile track that, its promotional material said, meant that there would be no need to relocate sewers, water pipes, electric, phone, Cablevision cables and so on, below the tram track. The shallow excavation would, it was suggested, lead to considerable cost saving and much less disruption in general – something that would hamper progress and increase costs on the tramway that was eventually built. A mock-up of a section of a lightweight car was displayed to the public in 1995 at Leith and in Parliament Square in the city centre. This carried Powergen and Pullman TPL branding, and by 1998 a working prototype was testing in Blackpool. Adoption of this lightweight system for Edinburgh was promoted by what was now the New Edinburgh Tramway Company (NET) as a lighter and cheaper alternative to the 'complex, weighty and expensive' cars produced by German builders. The 22-tonne (21.65-ton) trams would be 29m (95.14ft) long, carrying 80 seated and 120 standing passengers. This plan was rejected by the council, although a quarter of a century later Edinburgh trams would eventually cover much of the suggested route.

Then there were plans to build the east–west line as a guided busway, City of Edinburgh Rapid Transit (CERT). It was suggested that by 1999, this would connect Edinburgh Airport and a new park & ride facility at Ingliston with the city centre using the existing West Approach Road. However, this scheme collapsed in 2000 when the preferred bidder, FirstBus, pulled out just before construction started. Eventually a short (1.5km [$\frac{9}{10}$ mile]) section of guided busway between Saughton and South Gyle Access was opened in 2004, variously renamed WEBS (West Edinburgh Busway System) and Edinburgh Fastlink. This used Lothian buses fitted with guidewheels and only lasted until January 2009, as the guided section formed part of the new tramway that was in build by that time.

The council had wanted to pay for the proposed tramway and other improvements in the city by introducing congestion charging with inner and outer cordons. The people of Edinburgh were invited to participate in a referendum in 2005; from nearly 180,000 votes, the citizens voted roundly three to one against charging, so that income stream was no longer available.

Sitting on a stretch of disused dock railway track in July 1995, the mock-up of a section of a lightweight car is within sight of the Scottish government's main administrative building at Victoria Quay in Edinburgh.

Wearing Pullman and Powergen logos, the dummy tram was later on view in Parliament Square, in the centre of Edinburgh.

LEFT: The cover of a leaflet produced by the Edinburgh Tram Company promoting a light rail tramway that would follow a route between Haymarket and Newhaven, similar to the tramway that was eventually opened in 2023.

RIGHT: The New Edinburgh Tramways Company (NET) proposed a Haymarket-Newhaven tramway using lightweight trams and lighter track that could be laid directly in the road without the need to divert underground services.

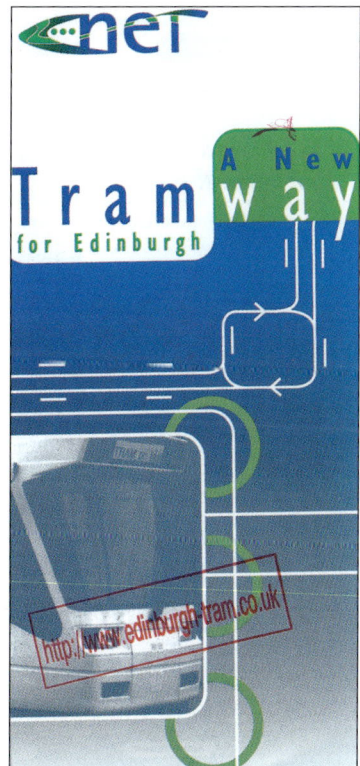

If older Edinburgh citizens were hoping that the city's 21st-century trams would look like the stately double-deck trams they remembered in constant procession in Princes Street, they were to be sorely disappointed. The appearance of a section of the prototype for the Bombardier cars for Nottingham Express Transit – another NET – set the record straight. Displayed in a marquee in East Princes Street Gardens in 2005, it showed what new-generation trams could be like.

After much deliberation, in 2004, the Scottish Parliament authorised a tram network that was to be introduced in phases.

Edinburgh was going to get its new tramway. Or was it?

ABOVE: In October 2005, this mock-up of the Bombardier Incentro trams built for the Nottingham Express Transit system that had opened in 2004 was displayed in a marquee on Edinburgh's East Princes Street Gardens allowing locals to experience a modern tram.

OPPOSITE ABOVE: The 1.5km (9/10 mile)-long guided busway that opened in the west of Edinburgh in 2004 was served by Lothian Buses routes 2 and 22. In May 2007, two Volvo B7RLE/Wright Eclipses pass on the busway. The 'G' diamond and fleet number suffix indicates buses fitted with guidewheels for this section of route. The busway closed in 2009 to allow for construction of the tram route on this section.

OPPOSITE BELOW: Track from Edinburgh's new tramway in the course of construction in March 2010, following the route used by the Fastlink busway, represented by the bus shelter on the left.

Signs of the Trams 1 – First Time Around in Leith

Right from the start, there were confident signs that the trams were coming to Leith. Most of these signs appeared in 2008–09, 15 years before the new trams would actually travel down Leith Walk. The future vision of Ocean Terminal suggests a three-track tramstop, which was never to materialise. The knitted 'Leith Says No To Trams' sign was placed in Leith Walk in 2019, around the time work was due to start nearby.

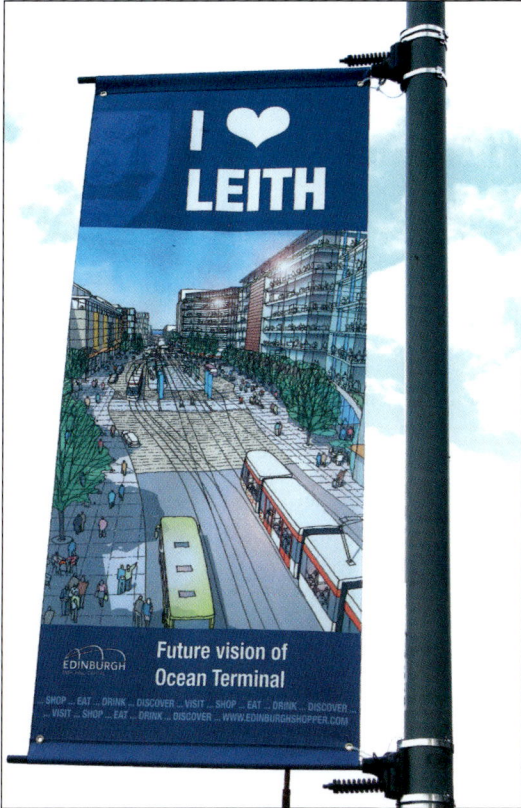

I ❤ LEITH

Future vision of
Ocean Terminal

... SHOP ... EAT ... DRINK ... DISCOVER ... VISIT ... SHOP ... EAT ... DRINK ... DISCOVER ...
... VISIT ... SHOP ... EAT ... DRINK ... DISCOVER ... WWW.EDINBURGHSHOPPER.COM

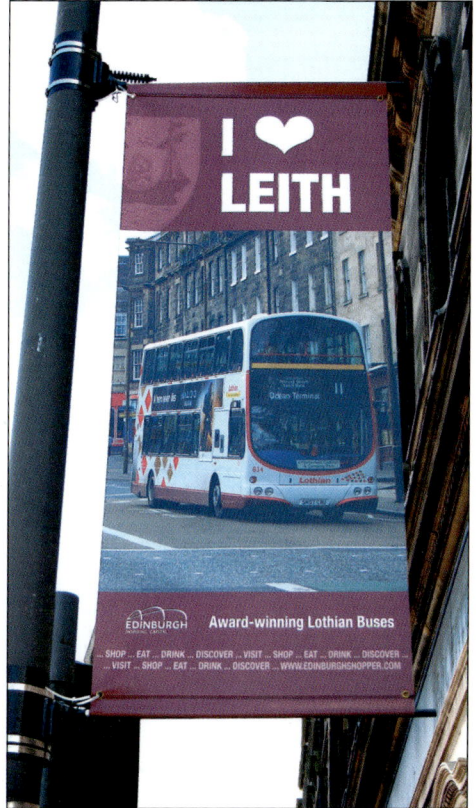

I ❤ LEITH

Award-winning Lothian Buses

... SHOP ... EAT ... DRINK ... DISCOVER ... VISIT ... SHOP ... EAT ... DRINK ... DISCOVER ...
... VISIT ... SHOP ... EAT ... DRINK ... DISCOVER ... WWW.EDINBURGHSHOPPER.COM

LEITH SAYS NO TO TRAMS

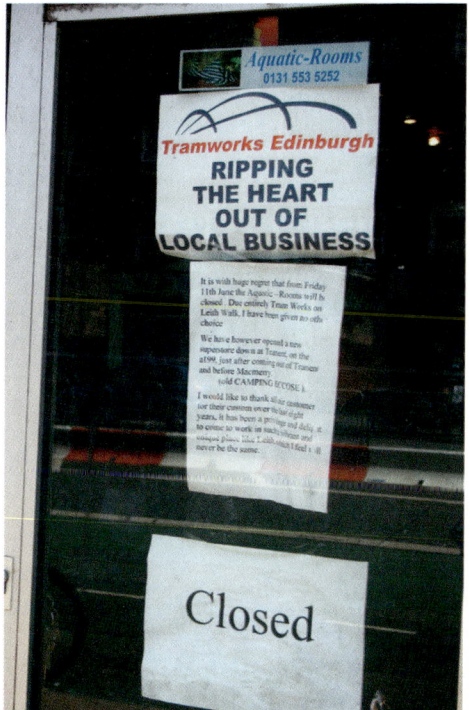

Aquatic-Rooms
0131 553 5252

Tramworks Edinburgh
RIPPING
THE HEART
OUT OF
LOCAL BUSINESS

Closed

Chapter 2

A Difficult Birth

The first street signs notifying locals that tramworks might cause diversions appeared in 2007 and advised that in connection with the Edinburgh Tram Project, there would be major roadworks on Leith Walk. Drivers were advised to use an alternate route as delays were possible. As drivers and pedestrians would soon discover, this seriously understated the impact of the tramworks.

One of the first indications of what was to come was this sign displayed at the east end of Princes Street in 2007. The Volvo B7RLE on the left is on the high-frequency 22 route that would be cut back when the tramway system eventually opened.

A Difficult Birth

In 1996, the City of Edinburgh Council (CEC) became the local government body for the city and had signalled its interest in reintroducing trams to the city. By 2003, things were beginning to progress and CEC was noting that the Scottish Executive was prepared to commit £375m to cover construction of a tramway. Transport Initiatives Edinburgh (Tie), owned by CEC, had been set up in 2002 and was tasked with various projects, including the new Edinburgh Trams.

A 2004 map of the proposed network, issued by Tie, illustrated the three-phase approach to introducing the new system. Phase 1A would be 18.5km (11½ miles) long and would connect Edinburgh Airport in the west of the city, through suburbs towards the city centre and then head north through Leith to a terminus at Newhaven. Phase 1B would be a connection west of Haymarket leading to a line heading north, mainly using existing walkways, to Granton Square on the shores of the Firth of Forth. Phase 2 would connect the Granton Square and Newhaven termini, a short distance with just one tramstop in-between, and Phase 3 would extend the tramway west from the Ingliston Park & Ride stop to Ratho and Newbridge.

In 2004, the French-based international public transport operator Transdev was chosen to operate the Edinburgh tramway, but its contract was terminated in 2009 in an effort to control ever-rising costs. A new company, Edinburgh Trams Ltd, assumed the operating role; this is a wholly-owned subsidiary of Transport for Edinburgh, in which CEC has a controlling interest.

By 2005, the estimate for the construction, trams and other infrastructure had risen to £539m purely for the Edinburgh Airport–Newhaven section, and rumblings about the ballooning costs led to the shelving of the Ingliston–Newbridge and Granton–Newhaven sections. There was still, CEC said, the optional extension on the Haymarket and Granton corridor, which might not proceed 'in the event that capital costs do not lie within a comfortable funding headroom'.

The Scottish National Party was now in control at CEC, and there was a strong possibility in 2007 that the whole project would be shelved, but by the end of the year contracts had been signed with what became known as the BSC consortium – Bilfinger Berger and Siemens for design and construction and CAF (Construcciones y Auxiliar de Ferrocarriles, based in Beasain, Spain) for the supply of 27 trams.

This allowed work to start in 2008, with underground utilities being moved in Leith Walk and Constitution Street. The locals got their first taste of the diversions and delays that would become increasingly familiar and

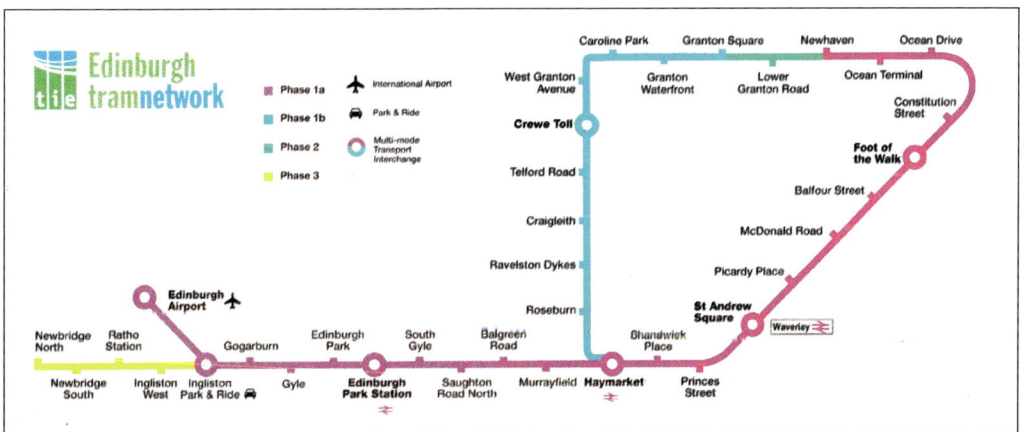

Transport Initiatives Edinburgh (Tie) produced this map of the tram network that was originally envisaged. The Edinburgh Airport–Newhaven section was eventually completed in 2023, and other sections – to Newbridge North, between Haymarket and Granton Square, and the Granton–Newhaven link, are still possible future projects.

The scene at the Foot of Leith Walk in April 2008 as work proceeded to prepare for the first line, which was initially planned to cover the entire route between the Airport and Newhaven, but the section beyond York Place through Leith had been abandoned by 2012 and only opened in 2023. The building with the prominent clock tower was part of the massive Leith Central railway station that had been opened in 1903 but closed to passengers in 1952.

irritating over the next few years. The irony was that the disruption to Leith and its businesses was unnecessary at this stage, as the Leith Walk to Newhaven section was abandoned in 2010 as costs spiralled, with the line stopping at York Place, just east of the city centre. As a city councillor remarked at the time: 'I don't know what the people of Edinburgh are going to make of it. They are only going to get half a tram line for far more than the original budget. When you look at the turmoil that has been caused in Leith and the anguish that shopkeepers have suffered, people are going to be absolutely livid when they hear what is happening now.' Another councillor added: 'All the digging and disruption on Leith Walk and in Leith has been a total waste of time and money'. Trams would eventually continue to Leith in 2023, which has helped the local economy, blighted by 15 years of disruption, delay and doubt.

As the great majority of the construction work on the tramway west of Haymarket to the Airport was not on existing roadways, it could progress with the minimum of inconvenience to the public. But the city centre section, from Haymarket rail station east towards Princes Street, St Andrew Square and York Place, would cause major disruption for some time, with Princes Street, the city's best-known street with shops on the north side and unrivalled views towards the Old Town and Edinburgh Castle on the south side, was closed to all traffic for long periods. From March 2009, during one of these closures, a mock-up of the trams being built by CAF in Spain was on display in Princes Street to give passers-by the opportunity to get a glimpse of what was – eventually – coming. More than 74,000 visitors (possibly 140,000, according to an official source) visited the mock-up before it was moved to be displayed in Leith and it now acts as an information bureau at the airport tram terminus.

A queue of Lothian and First buses gathers in Charlotte Square in May 2008 as traffic was diverted away from Princes Street during the tramworks.

With bus routes diverted away from Princes Street during tramworks in March 2009, this sign helped passengers find the nearest bus stop.

This view looking west along Princes Street in March 2009 captures the sheer scale of the work being undertaken.

Not the warmest of welcomes in 2009 for locals, shoppers and visitors with Princes Street closed off, while Edinburgh Castle rises above the restrictions.

A photo that says it all, with the Scott Monument silhouetted against a bright winter sky in 2009.

With Princes Street closed to traffic in 2009, the mock-up of the new trams offered a glimpse of the future.

Excavations, in October 2009, revealed the remains of the tunnel that housed the underground cables that propelled the cable cars running across Princes Street between Hanover Street and The Mound 90 years earlier. (Keith McGillivray)

LEFT: Princes Street reopened to buses – temporarily – in November 2009 and this notice guided potential passengers to the appropriate stops.

BELOW LEFT: There were problems with the track originally laid in Princes Street, requiring some to be relaid. This December 2009 view highlights the problem.

BELOW RIGHT: There were low-tech attempts, in April 2011, to fix the problem.

In the background, there were concerns over ever-rising costs and continuing conflicts over construction issues between CEC and its contractors. There were regular disagreements between Transport Initiatives Edinburgh, which was masterminding the project, and the contractors over rising costs and construction issues. The contractors pointed to a failure to divert utilities in time for tracks to be laid as unexpected obstacles were uncovered. There were periods over the next two years when all construction was stopped, and when there were public calls to scrap the whole project before it was too late. In fact, it was already too late, and it was pointed out that the cost of scrapping would be £750m, while completing the first stage of the tramway would cost £773m, which turned out to be roughly the figure that was spent, so there was no going back. And there was pressure from some quarters to stop the line at Haymarket, rather than continuing the tramway along the on-street section by Princes Street to York Place. Others argued that it could be sensible to *start* the tramway at Haymarket and run it through the city centre to Leith and Newhaven, as this would cover some of the most densely-populated areas in Edinburgh – indeed in Scotland – but a tramway to the airport was an important aim and, anyway, the tram depot was being built at Gogar, just a few stops away from the airport. And while these problems were dominating the local headlines, the first of the 27 trams ordered from CAF arrived in the city in 2010.

In the years between 2008 and 2012, while construction work and preparation for construction work was carried out, Princes Street was closed to all traffic for long periods, including the whole of 2009 and then again in 2011–12 as tracks were relaid, with the inevitable necessity to divert traffic on to other city centre streets and the consequent negative impact on local businesses. There were unexpected problems, too, such as the need to relay the concrete on the section between Shandwick Place and Haymarket, which had been closed to traffic for more than a year in 2012–13.

The depot for Edinburgh's new trams is situated at Gogar, just a few stops from the airport. It is in the build stage in April 2011.

Trams 254 and 270 inside the impressive Gogar Depot maintenance facility in August 2013.

A banner at Haymarket in June 2011 promotes the first line as originally planned, from the airport to Newhaven, which would initially be cut back to York Place (not on original map) and only opened to Newhaven in 2023.

A September 2011 sign in Princes Street warns that the road will be closed to traffic for many months.

Beyond the city centre, the work building the new tramway could proceed more smoothly and cause less disruption as it was mostly away from busy roads. This is the March 2012 view from Edinburgh Park Station looking back towards the city centre and Arthur's Seat. Work has commenced on the tramway alignment, straight ahead to the right of the railway.

ABOVE LEFT: A view looking west along Shandwick Place towards Haymarket, showing tram work in progress in April 2012.

ABOVE RIGHT: Tracklaying at the junction of Princes Street and South St Andrew Street in August 2012. The monument to Sir Walter Scott, the Edinburgh-born writer, dominates the view.

Tramworks at the usually busy junction of Princes Street, Shandwick Place and Queensferry Street in August 2012, with pedestrians corralled behind metal fencing.

The work on laying the track leading from Princes Street into South St Andrew Street, viewed from the Scott Monument in October 2012 as a Lothian Buses Alexander Dennis Enviro400H diesel-electric hybrid threads its way between the barriers. (Keith McGillivray)

While work progressed from Haymarket towards the city centre, buses followed tortuous diversions. This Lothian Airlink Volvo B9TL crosses West Maitland Street into Palmerston Place in March 2013 on its way to the airport.

While track was being laid, York Place was closed to traffic other than buses accessing the bus station. This First Alexander Dennis Enviro300 sets off on its long journey to Carlisle in March 2013.

Shandwick Place, leading to Princes Street, during tramworks in March 2013. The To Let signs indicate how businesses on this usually busy street were affected by the drop in footfall during this time.

Signage promoting the Airport–Newhaven line started appearing, promising trams by 2011, but it would be 12 more years before passengers would be able to travel by tram as far as Newhaven. In spite of the proposals to terminate Line 1A at Haymarket, Princes Street had to be served so St Andrew Square in the city centre became the preferred eastern terminus, abandoning the Leith–Newhaven section altogether. The track plans indicated that the nearest crossover to St Andrew Square would be a short distance further east, at York Place, and while it was only originally intended as a short spur purely to access the crossover, a passenger platform was created and York Place became the initial city terminus. Work on the section north to Leith was abandoned, which was a blow to the residents and businesses in Leith and Newhaven that had endured years of disruption for a tramway that it seemed might never be built.

In 2011, Tie, which was project-managing the new tramway, was closed down and the responsibility passed to Transport for Edinburgh, the organisation overseeing on-street public transport in the city. This allowed the building of Line 1A to proceed – late and over-budget – towards its opening to the public on 31 May 2014.

A promotional postcard anticipates the first trams in 2011, three years earlier than the actual opening of Line 1. The 'tram' is a mock-up produced to show passengers what modern trams would look like, liveried in the Harlequin style worn by Lothian Buses but not adopted for the actual trams.

RIGHT: A June 2013 sign informs passers-by that the Edinburgh Tram Network is being constructed by the Bilfinger Siemens Consortium.

BELOW: CAF Urbos 100 Trams pass near the Ingliston Park & Ride stop during pre-service tests in August 2013, wearing the original livery with a red flash above the side windows.

Signs warn pedestrians and motorists that tram testing is under way in February 2014; tram 267 prepares to cross the busy South Gyle Broadway.

You wait ages for a tram and then three come at once! Admittedly, it was unusual to find three trams on test in close proximity to each other, as here around the Edinburgh Park station in April 2014, just weeks before Line 1 opened to the public.

Tram 273 pauses at the Haymarket stop during testing in April 2014. The busy tramstop here would become an important interchange with buses, express coaches and the main rail line west from Edinburgh Waverley station.

ABOVE LEFT: A sign in York Place in May 2014, just ten days before the start of passenger service, warns pedestrians to be aware of the trams now testing over the full initial route between York Place and the airport.

ABOVE RIGHT: With the opening day of the Airport–York Place line approaching in 2014, tram 275 carries prominent vinyls to announce the date to the Edinburgh public. Here it heads west from the Haymarket stop a week before the trams were ready to roll.

This had been a massive undertaking for the City of Edinburgh Council, and the many difficulties faced before the trams carried a single fare-paying passenger were a hard-learned lesson that meant that the eventual construction of the continuation of the first line from York Place north towards Newhaven would progress much more smoothly and within budget. There would still be the inevitable disruption and there would still be anti-tram feeling among Edinburgh's citizens, but the public was now regularly updated about how the construction was progressing, and soon many would be won over by seeing and travelling on the trams. Now the council was already considering extensions to the south of the city.

The local newspaper, the *Edinburgh Evening News*, reflected on the ups and downs of the tram project from day one, and the next chapter is a reminder of the public mood during the most difficult building stages.

Car manufacturers are not usually great supporters of public transport, but this Kia dealership beside the tracks welcomes the trams on the first day of public service, 31 May 2014.

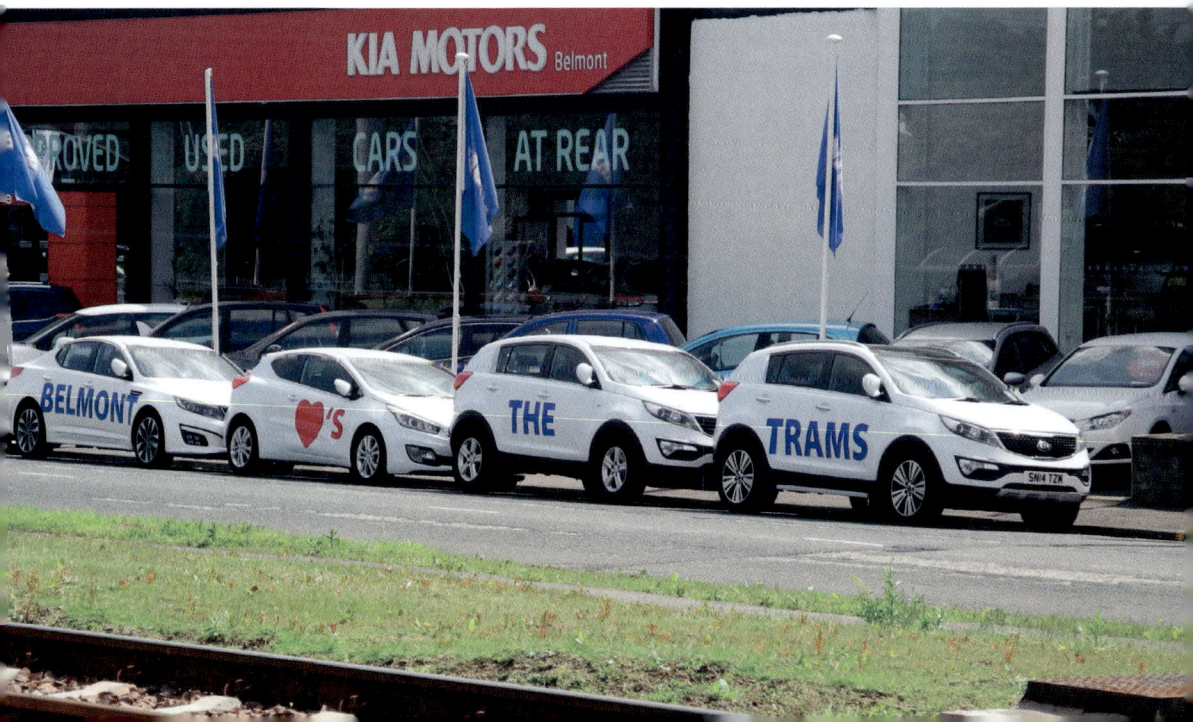

Signs of the Trams 2 – For and Against

The strength of feeling about the reintroduction of trams in Edinburgh is captured by these signs that appeared between the start of construction in 2009 through to the trams entering service between the airport and York Place and later. Most are self-explanatory – but the Tramway takeaway shopfront interestingly featured an early London tram; the print shop on the tram route in West Maitland Street was a particularly vocal and visual critic of the new trams, although visitors to Amsterdam, Helsinki, Munich and Prague might argue that the trams in these places are a successful and integral part of these cities; and the banner on a Shandwick Place bar intriguingly showed an Edinburgh cable car being hauled by two horses.

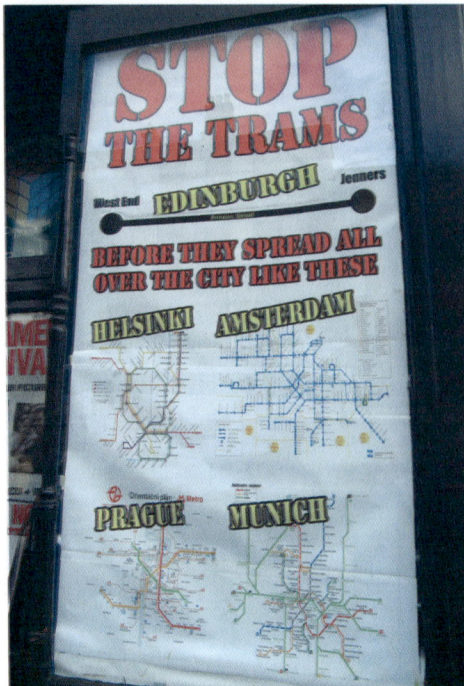

COMING SOON TO A STREET NEAR YOU !
a further epic five years in the making.
Brought to you by, and featuring
THE CITY OF EDINBURGH COUNCIL

Tramspotting. 2

A £207,000000 DARK COMEDY SEQUEL TO Tramspotting. 1
The £1 BILLION BUSINESS BUSTING HORROR!

With just 8 stops from York Place to Newhaven
this is a service for only the fit and able!.

Trams carry 250 passenger but only 78 seated
& 170 standing! only 2 wheelchair spaces.

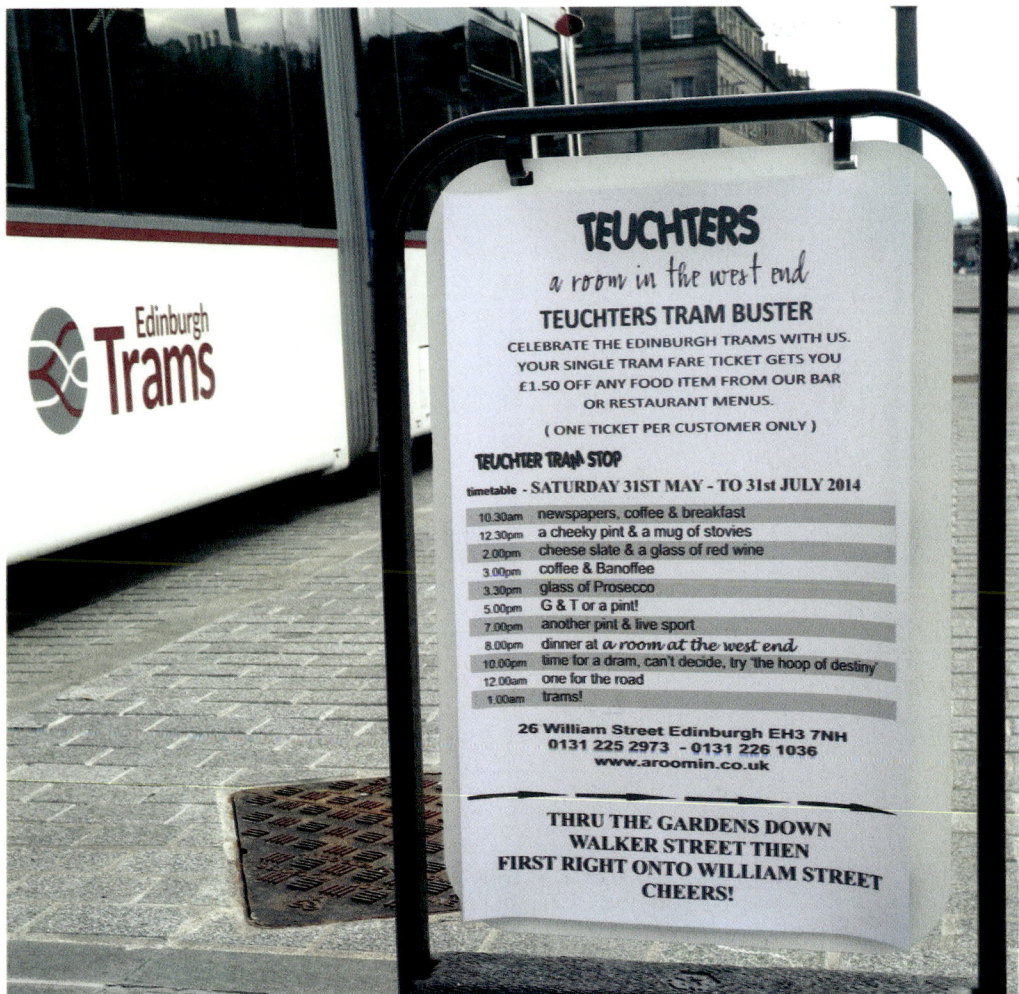

Edinburgh
Trams

TEUCHTERS
a room in the west end
TEUCHTERS TRAM BUSTER
CELEBRATE THE EDINBURGH TRAMS WITH US.
YOUR SINGLE TRAM FARE TICKET GETS YOU
£1.50 OFF ANY FOOD ITEM FROM OUR BAR
OR RESTAURANT MENUS.

(ONE TICKET PER CUSTOMER ONLY)

TEUCHTER TRAM STOP

timetable - SATURDAY 31ST MAY - TO 31st JULY 2014

10.30am	newspapers, coffee & breakfast
12.30pm	a cheeky pint & a mug of stovies
2.00pm	cheese slate & a glass of red wine
3.00pm	coffee & Banoffee
3.30pm	glass of Prosecco
5.00pm	G & T or a pint!
7.00pm	another pint & live sport
8.00pm	dinner at a room at the west end
10.00pm	time for a dram, can't decide, try 'the hoop of destiny'
12.00am	one for the road
1.00am	trams!

26 William Street Edinburgh EH3 7NH
0131 225 2973 - 0131 226 1036
www.aroomin.co.uk

THRU THE GARDENS DOWN
WALKER STREET THEN
FIRST RIGHT ONTO WILLIAM STREET
CHEERS!

Chapter 3

Hold the Front Page!

The local daily newspaper, the *Edinburgh Evening News*, has followed the city's tram saga from the start, cataloguing the ups and downs, the political involvement, the problems with contractors, and the possibility that the whole project would be abandoned or at best that the route would be severely curtailed. It has reflected the views of citizens who were for and often against the reintroduction of trams. And it has highlighted the good and bad times in its pages – often its front pages.

In March 2003, it led with the headline 'Trams are coming back', with the Scottish Executive providing £375m to pay for the first two city lines; trams would be starting 'as soon as 2009'. But by October 2005, under the headline 'City ready to pull the plug on tram links', came the first suggestion that the proposed links to Newbridge and Granton Waterfront could be postponed, as indeed they were. By December 2008 it was 'full steam ahead' as the paper reported under the headline 'All Aboard!' that cash, pegged at £592m, was in place for two lines. 'Trams work could start in three weeks', read a March 2007 headline, and by October 2008 tramworks were being blamed for 'Edinburgh grinding to a halt'. In November 2008, it reported that Line 1B, a 5.6km (3½ mile) stretch between Roseburn and Granton, was being scrapped as costs continued to soar.

ABOVE LEFT: The tram works affected life (and death) in Edinburgh. This is a March 2009 news bill.

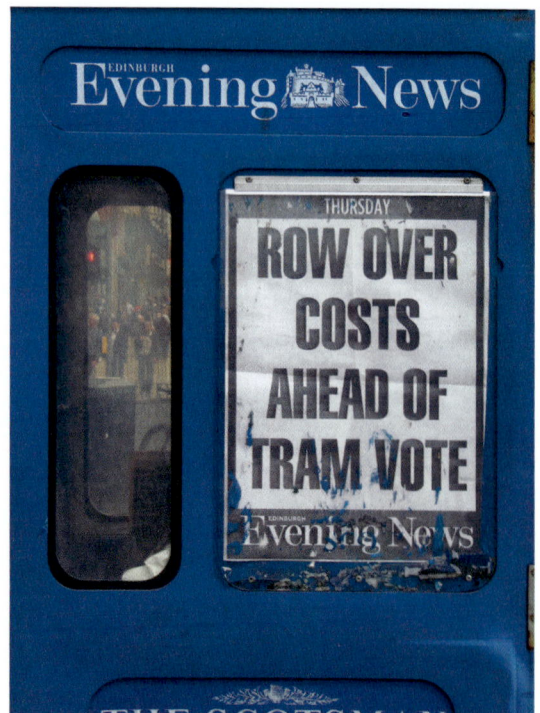

ABOVE RIGHT: This June 2011 news bill draws attention to the rising cost of the project.

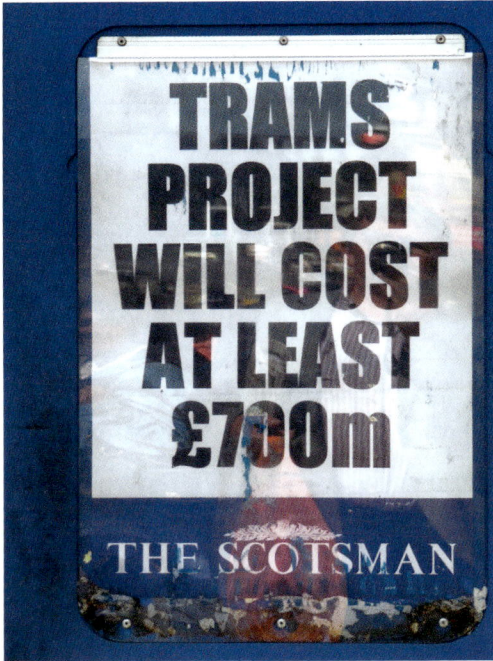

ABOVE LEFT: In June 2011, *The Scotsman* was also drawing attention to the ever-rising costs.

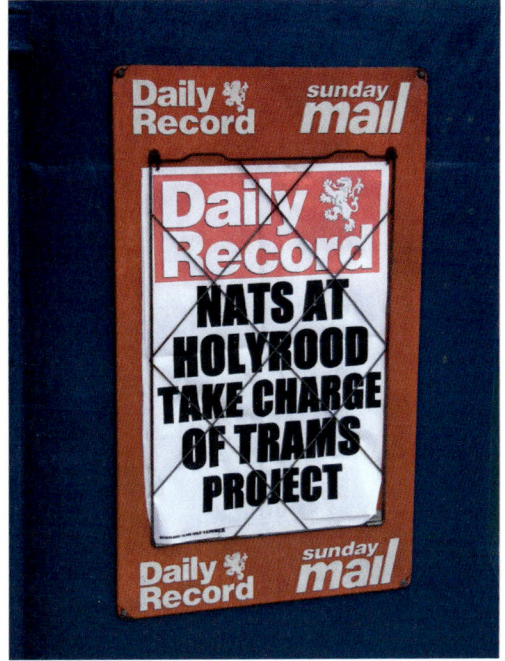

ABOVE RIGHT: The *Daily Record* reports in September 2011 that the Scottish National Party is taking control.

By 2009, there was a strong chance that Edinburgh would never get its new trams. The *News* reported that the tram line would not be ready until 2012, when 2011 had been the original target date. By October that year, it was reporting that costs would top £550m, and by June 2010 the headline 'Trams: End of the line' suggested that the worsening relations between the council and contractor Bilfinger Berger could signal the end of the project. The newspaper carried out a poll ('Trams split city') that revealed that 47 per cent wanted to scrap the trams and 39 per cent voted to keep the project going. In September 2010, the *News* revealed that York Place would be the terminus and that the continuation to Leith and Newhaven was to be shelved. But even that was in doubt; under the headline 'Last stop… Haymarket' the *News* reported that the council was actively considering curtailing the line at Haymarket, on the western fringes of the city centre, which would mean that Princes Street would not be served by the trams. A June 2011 poll revealed that 51.6 per cent wanted to 'Scrap them!' as a decision was awaited on continuing the line through the city centre, at a total cost for the project of £773m, but a month later the *News* admitted that 'despite our criticism of the management of the project over the years – and our close scrutiny will continue – it would be churlish not to acknowledge that the council made the right call in agreeing with the *News* that any line had to reach St Andrew Square'. The *News* concluded 'We now commend our latest advice to all those involved: OK, now get the damned thing built!'

By 2012, there was possibly a reluctant acceptance that the tram project would continue and the first line would link Edinburgh Airport in the west with York Place, on the east of the city centre, so the stories in the *News* majored less on the controversies and could report in January 2013 that 350 applications had been made for 12 jobs driving the trams ('Now we love the trams'), and in May 2013 that ambitious plans were being made to extend the tramway south into Midlothian ('Trams: Next stop Dalkeith'). The December 2013 headline

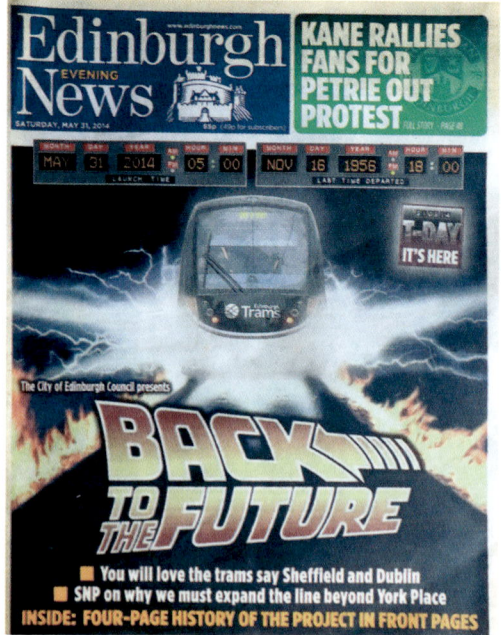

ABOVE LEFT: A positive *Edinburgh Evening News* front page in May 2013 anticipates services reaching the Royal Infirmary and into Midlothian at Dalkeith at some future stage.

ABOVE RIGHT: The big day at last, 31 May 2014, and the *News* gives the story the *Back to the Future* treatment.

On the day the new Edinburgh Trams went into service, the *News* reminds readers of the many front pages it has devoted to the tram project.

'57 years later' covered the first test journey of a tram along Princes Street since the final abandonment of the first-generation trams in 1956, and dubbed 31 May 2014 'T-Day', when the first public service started 'with no fanfare or ribbon-cutting'. The *News* front page read 'The City of Edinburgh Council presents Back to the Future', showing a new tram materialising in place of the DeLorean car in the movie.

Earlier in 2014, the *News* had provided a tongue-in-cheek feature ('Why capital trams are not so fast') listing major projects that had taken the same or rather less time to come to fruition than the seven years of the new Edinburgh trams – such as the Forth Bridge (also seven years), the Channel Tunnel (six years), the Eiffel Tower in Paris (two years) and the Empire State Building in New York (13 months). And a more positive attitude towards the trams was reflected in a front-page headline 'Council paves the way for trams to Leith' in March 2014 – two months before public service began between the airport and York Place – suggesting that 'City leaders will pave the way for an expansion of the route by "future proofing" improvement works in Leith Walk, where people have already endured prolonged disruption', and adding in a comment column that 'The move to extend trams to Leith in the next five years... largely depends on the success of the existing line and whether public opinion can be transformed. The early signs are good.' The line to and through Leith to Newhaven did indeed follow, though not in five years, but in nine. But it did follow.

A November 2021 *News* cover reveals that the Edinburgh Tram Inquiry has already taken longer than the Westminster government's Iraq War Inquiry.

Signs of the Trams 3 – The Trams are Coming

These photos taken between 2008 and 2023 show signs that kept the public advised of the progress of the tramway. These include warning and advisory signs, the ticket choices facing prospective passengers, and an intriguing (and short-lived) sign in Princes Street suggesting that trams would travel between Edinburgh and Cupar – the town more than 40 miles away across the Firth of Forth in Fife.

Chapter 4
The Trams

Edinburgh ordered 27 seven-section Urbos 100 cars from CAF. The first car, no.252, was delivered in April 2010 after a journey from the test-track in Wildenrath, Germany, by land and sea – in sections on a fleet of trucks – to Edinburgh. It was placed on public display in Princes Street, just west of The Mound, and although locals had seen the mock-up and had seen images of what the cars would look like, this was the first opportunity to sample the real thing. Some 140,000 people (74,000, according to another official source) inspected tram 252 while it was in Princes Street during its seven-month stay. For a day in September 2010, it had been moved further west, out of the way, in time for the visit of Pope Benedict XVI, but was soon returned to its original site. And during its residency in Princes Street, the original bright red flash above the side windows was replaced by one in the *weinrot* colour used by Lothian Buses.

ABOVE: The Spanish builder CAF won the contract to build Edinburgh's 27 new trams, and one features anonymously in this 2009 advert, using an artist's impression of one of the Edinburgh cars in the Harlequin livery that was not adopted. The Scott Monument in Princes Street is reflected in the driver's windscreen.

OPPOSITE ABOVE: The first complete tram to be seen in Edinburgh was no.252, which arrived in sections on Dutch trucks. Here the trucks assemble on Regent Road on the evening of 25 April 2010. All other trams were delivered directly to the tram depot at Gogar. (Keith McGillivray)

BELOW: Later the same evening, 252 was taken for assembly to Princes Street where it was to be on display to the public against the backdrop of Edinburgh Castle. It remained in situ until November 2010. (Keith McGillivray)

LEFT: The assembled 252 was on display to the public on the tram tracks in Princes Street, adjacent to West Princes Street Gardens. A month after it arrived, the red flash above the side windows was altered to the *weinrot* colour used by Lothian Buses. The statue on the left remembers Allan Ramsay, the 18th-century portrait painter.

BELOW: Sitting among traffic in Princes Street at what would become the Princes Street tramstop, 252 in August 2010, now with its *weinrot* flash.

This word cloud displayed inside 252 summarises the frequency of the words used in feedback by visitors to the tram.

The 42.8m-long (140.42ft) trams have space for 250 passengers, 78 of them seated, and as the first route terminates at Edinburgh Airport, there is a significant amount of luggage space provided. The double-ended cars have doors on both sides as the tramstops are a mix of side and central platforms.

The last of the 27 trams, no.269, reached Edinburgh in December 2012, joining the others at Gogar Depot. Initially, barely a dozen of the 27-strong fleet would be needed for the service and there had been a suggestion that, as Edinburgh had too many trams for the Airport–York Place route, some of the surplus trams might be leased to Transport for London's Croydon Tramlink, but this suggestion was never taken up. The fact that the Edinburgh trams are 42.8m (more than 140ft) long and the Croydon trams are 32.4m (more than 106ft) long may have influenced this decision.

The trams were delivered to and assembled at Gogar Depot and started test running between the depot and Edinburgh Park Station tramstop in October 2010. Tram testing reached as far into the city as Haymarket by December 2013 and on the fifth of that month, tram 254 was tested around midnight on-street all the way to York Place for the first time, at walking pace. There were also overnight tests at line speed on Princes Street, with all side roads closed off.

The first daytime appearance of a tram in the city centre was when tram 265 was displayed at the St Andrew Square stop along with a Lothian bus, for the launch of Transport for Edinburgh in December 2013. It then proceeded slowly back to the depot, pausing at the Princes Street tramstop, which attracted much public attention. Two months later, tram 255 was used for the first formal daytime on-street testing, and the following

Trams in the yard at Gogar Depot in July 2012, all but one displaying the original red flash. No.252 with its *weinrot* flash also has an Edinburgh Inspiring Capital logo on the front.

On the night of 5 December 2013, tram 254 made a journey to the end of the line at York Place, moving at walking pace to identify any issues – the first journey on public roads. Here it turns from York Place into North St Andrew Street as it makes its slow return journey to Gogar Depot. (Keith McGillivray)

A rare sight – two Edinburgh trams coupled together, stretching for 85.6m (281ft in old money!) along York Place on 12 February 2014, testing the ability of one tram to rescue another in the event of a breakdown. (Keith McGillivray)

month, 266 was used to test crowd evacuation from the Murrayfield Stadium stop. There was also a brief appearance of two trams coupled together, testing the feasibility of rescuing a broken-down tram.

A largely white livery was chosen, with a coloured band above the side windows; at first this was bright red, but soon the *weinrot* colour was adopted. Initially, trams with both versions of the livery could be seen in service, but the bright red soon disappeared and a decade later the trams now wear advertising liveries, some superimposed on the white base, and others covering the entire tram – even over some of the side windows at times.

Although fewer than half of Edinburgh's 27 trams were needed for the 2014-introduced Airport–York Place section, the June 2023 opening of the extension to Newhaven has made good use of the entire fleet with improved frequencies, and as you pass Gogar Depot now you will see fewer trams sitting in the sidings.

RIGHT: The seven-section 42.8m (140.42ft)-long CAF Urbos 100s for Edinburgh have space for 250 passengers, 78 seated. Note the red Edinburgh Trams logo on the seats.

BELOW: The first daylight appearance of a new tram running in Princes Street was on 17 December 2013, when 265 was involved in the launch of Transport for Edinburgh and here it pauses at the Princes Street tramstop on its return journey to Gogar Depot.

Signs of the Trams 4 – Lessons learned

The tramway extension from York Place to Newhaven produced its own selection of official signs as it was clear Edinburgh Trams had learned lessons from the problems encountered with the Airport–York Place line and worked hard to keep locals advised about what was happening and when. The personalised manhole cover is interesting, as is the unofficial Banksy-style mural on a corner wall in Jane Street, adjacent to the Leith Walk tramway.

The Rebel Bear

* Trams Currently Being Tested *
Trams to Leith, Ocean Terminal and
Newhaven COMING SOON
11:31:25

The Trams to Newhaven construction sites comply with Scottish Government guidance on working safely as a result of COVID-19.

Further information can be found at www.tramstonewhaven.co.uk or you can contact us by

Email:
Newhaven.tram@edinburgh.gov.uk

Phone:
0131 322 1122

www.tramstonewhaven.co.uk

EDINBURGH TRAMS

DING DING

Airport 953

Edinburgh Trams

Chapter 5

To York Place, Newhaven – and Beyond

On Saturday 31 May 2014, packed tram 275 provided the first journey for paying passengers, leaving the Gyle Centre and heading for York Place, and over the next days and weeks locals and enthusiasts flocked to the tramstops to see and sample what they had been waiting for since 2008. Had the diversions and disruptions been worth it? Opinion at the time was divided, and there are still those who think the project should never have gone ahead. But passenger numbers grew from 5.2 million in 2015, the first full year of operation, to 7.45m in 2019, before the inevitable drop during the Covid pandemic in 2020–21, which seriously affected public transport journeys in Edinburgh, as they did throughout the UK. The numbers bounced back in 2022, and in 2023, which included almost seven months of the full Airport–Newhaven route, the figures jumped to 9.3m, with the festival month of August being the busiest, accounting for 1.2m passengers.

The initial public timetable for the start of the new trams in 2014 was based on an 8–10-minute frequency during the greater part of the day, Mondays to Saturdays, and with a scheduled single journey time of 39/40 minutes, only around 11 of the 27 trams would be in service at any time, although all 27 were used on a rotation basis. Single fares were £1.50 for the City Zone, which covered every stop except the last leg to the airport for which a premium of £5.00 was charged to passengers travelling beyond the Ingliston stop; the equivalent 2024 fares were £2 and £7.50.

It was clear that the hard-learned lessons from the painful saga of the Airport–York Place tramway would influence the building of the rest of Line 1, beyond York Place. The original options were terminating at the Foot of Leith Walk, or further to Ocean Terminal, or one stop even further to Newhaven. The decision was to extend to Newhaven and the work, starting in 2019, was carried out with much less disruption than before, and the public were kept informed about the progress so there was a much more positive attitude towards the new route. Although all of the construction work involved busy streets, including Leith Walk, which has one of the highest population densities in Scotland, the work was managed better, was delivered on time and within the budget of £207.3m – bringing the total costs for Line 1 to more than £1bn, twice the original estimate. The first overnight test of the Newhaven route was carried out on 23 March 2023, using tram 258, displaying appropriate vinyls, and the full service between Edinburgh Airport and Newhaven started on 7 June 2023.

An independent inquiry commissioned by the Scottish government into the protracted introduction and soaring costs of the trams, was set up in 2014, the year the Airport–York Place section first carried passengers, and the Edinburgh Tram Inquiry was concluded in 2023, costing more than £13m, roughly the same, it was pointed out, as the Chilcot Inquiry into the Iraq War. Chaired by Lord Hardie, a retired Court of Session Judge, it held hearings between 2015 and 2018 and the 960-page report was published in 2023.

Looking north down pre-tram Leith Walk in July 2014 with cars, taxis, vans and Lothian buses on this spacious boulevard. In the distance, across the Firth of Forth, is the Kingdom of Fife.

The view in March 2024, with the tram tracks in the centre of the street, and widened pavements and cycleways.

Edinburgh's New Trams

In his report Lord Hardie wrote:

What is clear from the inquiry's work is that there was a litany of avoidable failures on the parts of several parties whose role it was to ensure that public funding was spent effectively and to the benefit of Scotland's taxpayers, and that the Edinburgh Trams Project was delivered efficiently.

Poor management and abdication of responsibility on a large scale have had a significant and lasting impact on the lives and livelihoods of Edinburgh residents, and the reputation of the city.

The Leader of the City of Edinburgh Council responded:

While we broadly agree with Lord Hardie's recommendations, prior to the inquiry's announcement we had already introduced processes and strategies to help avoid some of the problems experienced in the original tram project. Not only have we applied this in the construction of the line to Newhaven, but these lessons are hugely beneficial to other major infrastructure projects.

Since the start of the Tram Inquiry, we've completed the line to Newhaven and launched passenger services, the success of which was down to the hard work of the in-house project team and partners. It's also thanks to lessons learned from the first project, and our own improvements to project management and governance, communication and independent oversight.

It's worth noting too, that in the nine years since the line between Edinburgh Airport and York Place was built, the service has flourished to become a hugely successful transport route for thousands of residents and visitors each day.

This was the largest capital project in living memory undertaken by CEC, and now the early mistakes are filed away as a warning to other authorities considering introducing new-generation trams. After all the disruption, the infighting, the secrecy, the blame game and the uncertainty that the project would ever be completed, Edinburgh has a successful and well-used first line, with significant extensions being seriously considered.

LEFT: In 2018, the city council was keen to consult with members of the public on the Trams to Newhaven project.

OPPOSITE ABOVE: May 2021 and the crossover is being installed at Ocean Terminal, just one stop short of the Newhaven terminus.

OPPOSITE BELOW: This is the tramstop at The Shore under construction in March 2022. The stop is just short of the busy junction at Bernard Street.

Foundations in place in July 2022 at Ocean Drive where the tramway curves right towards the Ocean Terminal shopping centre. On the left is the 1874 Victoria Swing Bridge, which carried road and rail traffic serving Leith Docks. Now Category A listed, it has been undergoing refurbishment.

The previous tramstop at York Place was closed when the Newhaven extension was in build, and its replacement is now at Picardy Place. The island platform, seen under construction in July 2022, now forms one part of a large one-way traffic triangle as the tracks lead north towards Leith. The 1929-built 3,000-seat Playhouse Theatre, now Category A listed, is in the background centre.

Work nears completion on the section of track linking Ocean Terminal with the Newhaven terminus in March 2023, just three months before the start of public service.

ABOVE LEFT: The first tram in Leith for 67 years was 258, uniquely carrying advertising promoting the trams to Newhaven. It is progressing at walking pace along Constitution Street towards Newhaven on the evening of 13 March 2023.

ABOVE RIGHT: Tram 273 heads east between the stops at Port of Leith and The Shore in May 2023, on pre-service testing a week before the start of public service.

RIGHT: The Picardy Place stop in May 2023 as work continues on the large traffic island to the right of the tram.

One part of the original planned tram route would have linked Roseburn, just east of the Murrayfield Stadium stop, and Granton, on the Firth of Forth, site of a £1.3bn regeneration programme, which includes thousands of new homes. From Granton this could be extended a fairly short distance to meet the Newhaven line. Another new route could be a line on the A71 corridor west towards the Heriot-Watt University complex. More ambitious proposals are a tramway continuing east along Princes Street and heading south by the North Bridge route towards the Royal Infirmary at the BioQuarter at Little France, and even to the Midlothian town of Dalkeith, with possibly a branch into East Lothian at Musselburgh. With Edinburgh's population projected to grow at three times the rest of Scotland's, and the city's aim to reduce car kilometres by 30 per cent to become a net zero city by 2030, an expanded tram network would play an important role in providing safe, efficient and affordable travel.

So, a happy ending after 'a litany of avoidable failures', to use the words of Lord Hardie that were picked up by many headline writers when his report was published. And in a city used to good-quality and well-used public transport provided by Lothian Buses and now Edinburgh Trams, the future looks bright – certainly considerably brighter than it did in the early years of this century.

Chapter 6
Enjoy the Journey

An end-to-end trip on the new trams is well worth it, offering glimpses of Edinburgh's many faces. The single fare from Edinburgh Airport to Newhaven at 2025 prices is £5.00, but the majority of passengers travelling east on the route between the Ingliston Park & Ride stop and Newhaven, one stop short of the airport, pay just £2.00, the same as a single fare on Lothian's city buses. Lothian does offer its round-the-clock Airlink bus service, with an adult single costing £5.50. Between the city centre and the airport, the tram and bus services follow different routes; the bus uses the direct A8 road and the tram covers areas to the south. Coming from the airport, our tram follows reserved track all the way to Haymarket, after which the airport trams and buses share the same streets between Haymarket and Princes Street. Our tram is timetabled to take 34 minutes for the trip between the airport and St Andrew Square, in the city centre. The bus is scheduled to take between 24 and 29 minutes off-peak, and up to 33 minutes at peak times, and although it has the advantage of bus lanes over much of its route, at times it is at the mercy of other traffic.

Visitors arriving at Edinburgh Airport are directed to the trams and the Airlink bus, with departure points within sight of each other. Potential passengers from other countries might be used to catching a tram to the city centre, while others might be attracted by the novelty of travelling upstairs on a double-deck bus. Tram passengers are greeted by the mock-up tram module that was used in 2009 to publicise the coming trams and is now an information point beside the tram terminus. A bank of ticket machines provides the necessary tickets and Edinburgh Trams' staff are on hand to help. Passengers can also download the Transport for Edinburgh (TfE) app to buy tram and bus tickets, or the ET App to buy tram tickets, including bundle deals, and can pre-purchase tickets online at edinburghticket.com. Single and day return fares covering all zones are available for adults and children (age 5–15), and there are equivalent fares for the City Zone, covering all stops except the final leg to the airport. Day tickets for the Airport Zone and City Zone are also available, and these cover bus and tram services. There are also fares covering the city zone for buses and trams – the LATEticket for travel after 18.00 and the Family DAYticket for up to two adults and up to three children. Passengers must board the trams with a valid ticket or pass, as tickets issued on-board are charged at a premium fare.

Travellers arriving at Edinburgh's busy airport are presented with a choice of travel modes for their journey into central Edinburgh. On the left is the tram terminus and on the right, the stop for the Lothian Buses 24-hour Airlink Express service.

The tram module mock-up that was displayed in Edinburgh and Leith before the new trams started to arrive is now the tramlounge by the airport tram terminus.

Tram 266 awaits passengers at the airport terminus in March 2024. The number 965 in the windscreen is a running number, with the tram's fleet number above the windscreen.

Trams use both platforms at the Edinburgh Airport terminus, and this July 2014 photo shows 277, the highest numbered tram, crossing to the island platform.

Tram 277 heads from the airport to Newhaven in March 2024 against the backdrop of airport hotels and the airport's iconic 57m-high Control Tower, opened in 2005. By this time, all trams carried external advertising liveries; some, like 277, retained much of the white livery on the lower panels, while others are completely wrapped with advertising.

A journey over the whole tram route to Newhaven is scheduled to take 54 minutes, running every seven minutes through most of the day. Our journey starts at the island-platform Edinburgh Airport terminus. Edinburgh is Scotland's busiest airport, handling 14.4m passengers a year on flights to more than 150 destinations. The main terminal building opened in 1977 and facilities have continued to expand since then. Tram passengers get some idea of the size of the airport as we start our journey passing hotels, walkways, car parks, car hire offices, the impressive 57m-tall Control Tower and the odd glimpse of the tailfin of a plane, as our tram heads towards the two-platform stop at Ingliston Park & Ride, the first of 21 tramstops before it reaches the Newhaven terminus. Our tram turns sharply left to reach the Ingliston stop, which is well-placed for car drivers approaching Edinburgh from the north and west, offering them the chance to park and take a 29-minute tram ride to Princes Street, in the heart of the city. The P&R facility is also served by Lothian's Skylink buses, catering for passengers travelling from the airport to other parts of the city, avoiding the central area. Passengers for events at the Royal Highland Centre, like the annual Royal Highland Show, can alight at the Ingliston stop for a 10–15-minute walk to the showground.

No.252 negotiates the sharp double bends between Ingliston and Gogarburn in July 2014. The diamond-shaped sign warns drivers that 20km/h (12.4mph) is the maximum speed around these bends.

City-bound 271 at the Ingliston Park & Ride stop in May 2016 showing the style adopted for many of the stops.

There is open land surrounding the Ingliston stop, but there are signs of groundwork for a new stop, which would serve future residential or commercial developments. A board at the Ingliston stop announces a coming housing project, West Town. Sharp right and left turns bring you to Gogarburn tramstop, convenient for the 90-acre NatWest Group Gogarburn House office and conference centre complex, opened by the Royal Bank of Scotland in 2005 and reached on foot by a bridge crossing the busy A8 road.

On its way to the next stop our tram skirts its depot at Gogar, a spacious site adjacent to the A8 and A720 (city bypass) roads. The depot provides extensive external sidings for the trams and the buildings contain the main offices and operational control centre as well as workshop areas, a tram wash area, maintenance pits and a testing area. Initially short platforms on the line to and from the airport, adjacent to the depot, were used for crew changes and access, but these can now be carried out at the next stop, Edinburgh Gateway. This stop was added in 2016 to provide interchange with the adjacent (at a higher level) rail lines north from Edinburgh towards the Forth Bridge. This extravagant structure provides covered platforms for the trams – the only tramstop with full cover – and there are escalators up to the train station, which connect the tramway with trains to Perth, Dundee and the Fife Circle, aimed particularly at passengers from the north heading to Edinburgh Airport, but passenger figures using the interchange have been disappointing.

An advertising hoarding at the Ingliston stop in March 2024 features a tram as it announces plans to create the new West Town neighbourhood on land adjacent to the airport.

A pastoral scene approaching the Gogarburn stop – 272 in July 2014.

In March 2023, 265 drifts into the Gogarburn stop, handy for staff and visitors to the former Royal Bank of Scotland campus to the left across the busy A8 road; the footbridge with the RBS logo connects the office complex to the tramstop. Note the St Andrew Square tramboard behind the windscreen. These were not always changed at termini, but this one is correct.

ABOVE: Gogarburn stop in March 2024 and doors are closed as the driver of 277 prepares to continue the journey to Newhaven.

RIGHT: Between Gogarburn and Edinburgh Gateway stops, the service trams skirt the Gogar Depot. In this July 2014 shot, 274 passes the depot yard with many other trams in evidence. The entire fleet of 27 trams is now necessary for the full service to Newhaven.

The 2016-opened Edinburgh Gateway stop provides interchange facilities for tram passengers with trains heading between Edinburgh and Fife, Perth, Dundee and Inverness. It is the only fully covered stop on the system and rail passengers use escalators in the dark-coloured building on the right to reach trains at the higher level. Trams at Gogar Depot can just be seen in the background as 276 heads to central Edinburgh.

Another sharp right-hand curve and the tramway passes under the A8 road and ascends towards the Gyle Centre stop, serving this important out-of-town shopping complex. Leaving this busy stop, our tram crosses South Gyle Broadway, the only significant road crossing on this section of the route before it reaches Haymarket. This takes us to Edinburgh Park, first opened in 1995, an attractively landscaped area that is home to corporate, often financial, businesses housed in buildings in a range of architectural styles, facing on to grassed areas that include a stream and a range of sculptures. The two-platform tramstop is Edinburgh Park Central. The tramway then proceeds across currently undeveloped land to a long left-curving viaduct over roadways and the main rail lines to the west. At the Edinburgh Park Station tramstop, there is interchange with trains towards Falkirk, Stirling, Dunblane and Glasgow, and with Lothian buses, as well as access to the Hermiston Gait retail park.

The popular Gyle Centre stop gives passengers access to the large shopping complex there. No.257 heads for York Place in December 2016.

Lights reflect in the wet platforms at Gyle Centre in December 2016.

A sunny day in July 2014 as 276 glides away from the Gyle Centre stop towards the airport.

RIGHT: An Airport-bound tram sits at the Edinburgh Park Central stop after crossing the bridge over the railway in March 2023. Note the sign reminding drivers of a pedestrian crossing.

BELOW: Sitting at the Edinburgh Park Central stop in March 2023, 276 is bound for St Andrew Square.

ABOVE LEFT: After crossing the railway, 276 descends towards Edinburgh Park Station in March 2023.

ABOVE RIGHT: Edinburgh Park Station provides direct interchange facilities with trains to and from the west of Scotland. No.259 sets off for the airport in June 2014.

LEFT: Looking eastward along the tram tracks from Edinburgh Park Station in March 2023, with Arthur's Seat in the background. This marks the end of a fast (70km/h [43.95mph]) stretch of track.

Enjoy the Journey

There follows a long straight stretch of fast (70km/h [43.95mph]) tramway towards central Edinburgh, with the railway to the left, with two-platform tramstops at Bankhead and Saughton, partly following the route of the 1.5km (0.93 mile) Edinburgh Fastlink guided busway that was served by Lothian buses between 2004 and 2009. This is the only section of route between the Airport and Haymarket where the tramway comes close to dense residential areas with easy access to the trams. And there are good views north towards Corstorphine Hill and Edinburgh Zoo, and south towards the Pentland Hills. At this point, the tramway has been running in parallel with the westbound railway lines and now it crosses the railway again, still running alongside the railway, to the tramstop at Balgreen, dominated by the building still prominently lettered 'Jenners Depository', a reminder of the once-familiar upmarket department store on Princes Street. This is another fast section of the tramway where line speeds of up to 70km/h (43.95mph) are permitted. Diamond-shaped signs on the overhead line poles advise the tram drivers of changes of speed, which range from 10km/h on sharp curves, to 25km/h for on-street sections up to 35, 40, 50 and 70km/h, depending on the terrain – that is a range from 6.2mph to 43.95mph.

RIGHT: Everything looks pristine for 258 at Bankhead tramstop in April 2014, just over a month before the start of public service.

BELOW: Tram 276, wrapped overall for the energy supplier OVO, at Bankhead stop in March 2024. The pink validator to the left is for passengers with concession and other passes.

ABOVE: The Saughton tramstop in April 2014, with a tram on a test run just weeks away from the opening of the Airport–York Place section.

LEFT: Diamond-shaped signs warn drivers of a pedestrian crossing and the 40km/h (24.85mph) speed limit on the descent to Saughton stop. No.267 in July 2023.

In service in July 2014, Airport-bound 268 has crossed the railway on its way to the Saughton stop.

On test in March 2014, this tram is about to cross the railway tracks between Saughton and Balgreen.

RIGHT: With an ominous sky in the distance, this tram has crossed the railway bridge in December 2017, next stop Balgreen.

BELOW: In April 2014, with full-route testing underway, 272 and 251 pass Carrick Knowe housing.

ABOVE: In July 2014, 261, bound for the Airport, has run from the Balgreen stop in parallel with the westbound railway tracks and is now climbing to cross the railway towards the west. Edinburgh Castle dominates the background.

LEFT: The Balgreen stop is overlooked by the former Jenners Depository building as 275 sets off for the Airport in July 2014.

The next tramstop is one of the busiest, but only on certain days each year. It is Murrayfield Stadium, serving the home of Scottish rugby and the largest stadium in Scotland, the fifth largest in the United Kingdom. A substantial flight of steps takes rugby fans down from the tramway level directly to the stadium's entry gates. For rail fans, the tramway line skirts Haymarket train maintenance depot, once home to the most glamorous LNER Pacific steam locomotives, and now a diesel depot where you might catch a glimpse of the iconic InterCity trains, using upgraded Class 43 High-Speed Trains (HSTs). Beyond Murrayfield, there is a reminder on the left of what might have been – and what could be in the future: concrete groundwork for a tramway junction leading north towards Granton.

RIGHT: The view forward from 263 leaving the Murrayfield Stadium stop in July 2014, passing city-bound 256 with the stadium on the right.

MIDDLE: With Murrayfield Stadium on the right, a tram leaves the stop for the Airport in March 2024. The blue rosette on the tram celebrates the naming of Edinburgh Trams as Public Transport Operator of the Year.

BELOW: Between Murrayfield Stadium and Haymarket stops there is a reminder of what might have been – the concrete foundations for the yet-to-be-built extension to Granton. This is 261 heading for the Airport in June 2014.

Edinburgh's New Trams

Before the tramway curves away from the rail lines that run parallel and heads from its reserved track to on-street running at Haymarket, there is a siding, a short length of track, accessed from both main tram tracks, which is used to park extra trams that might be needed for sporting and other events at Murrayfield, and more generally elsewhere on the network. Past this, our tram slows for a sharp left turn and a slow winding climb up to a right-hand bend and Haymarket tramstop. This busy two-platform stop is adjacent to Haymarket railway station, the seventh busiest in Scotland. There is also direct interchange with local and longer-distance bus and coach services. Continuing on our way, our tram negotiates the busy Haymarket junction, now dominated by a prestigious office development, and starts its on-street section, which continues for the remainder of the route to Newhaven, largely following in the tracks of Edinburgh's first-generation tramway, abandoned almost 70 years earlier, in 1956.

LEFT: To the west of the Haymarket stop the tramway runs parallel with the railway on a 70km/h (43.95mph) stretch towards the Airport. In March 2024, 256 passes a siding that is used for extra trams at busy times, such as rugby internationals at Murrayfield Stadium.

BELOW: After following the route paralleling the main railway tracks, Newhaven-bound trams wend their way up to the Haymarket stop. No.256 in March 2024.

ABOVE: Haymarket tramstop in March 2024 with 256 bound for Newhaven. This stop marks the start of on-street running on the journey to the north. The railway station is on the right and includes the original Category A-listed 1842 building. The modern office complex that dominates the centre of this photo did not exist when trams started serving this stop in 2014.

RIGHT: Tram 262 pulls away from the Haymarket stop, heading for Newhaven in June 2018. The window firm CR Smith was the first commercial business to advertise on the trams.

Now our tram is surrounded by general road traffic as we head east towards Princes Street, between the twin Georgian buildings of Coates Crescent and Atholl Crescent, part of the western development of Edinburgh's New Town, to reach the West End island platform stop. Just west of this tramstop is a trailing crossover, allowing trams to terminate there during demonstrations and other events affecting Princes Street. There are also trailing crossovers at Gogar Depot, Edinburgh Park Station, Haymarket, York Place, Balfour Street and Ocean Terminal, and double crossovers at the Airport and Newhaven termini. West End is the third name for this stop; it was first Shandwick Place, then West End – Princes Street. As our tram proceeds along Shandwick Place, it passes the Travel Hub by Lothian on the right, providing information about the trams and Lothian's buses, and boasting a popular cafe.

ABOVE: The West End stop was previously known as West End – Princes Street, as in this July 2014 view of 277 bound for the Airport. The tower of the Charlotte Baptist Chapel is prominent in the background.

LEFT: The crossover in Shandwick Place is used for short workings and when trams can continue no further east because of processions and incidents. No.277 crosses from the eastbound track at the start of a journey to the Airport in December 2015.

Wearing an allover advert, 273 proceeds along Shandwick Place in November 2023, passing the Lothian Buses TravelHub providing information on Lothian Buses and Edinburgh Trams, which also includes a popular cafe.

Tram 254 crosses the junction with Queensferry Street as it heads from Shandwick Place into Princes Street in June 2018.

Looking south at the West End junction with Lothian Road in March 2024, 275 passes St John's Church on Princes Street, and offers views towards Edinburgh Castle, the spire of St Cuthbert's Church and a glimpse of the red sandstone of the Caledonian Hotel, before passing Rutland Place into Shandwick Place.

Edinburgh's New Trams

As our tram approaches Princes Street, there is a first glimpse of Edinburgh Castle to the right and we pass one of the two great railway hotels that bookend the street. The red sandstone Waldorf Astoria Edinburgh – The Caledonian, to give it its full name, was built by the Caledonian Railway and opened in December 1903 as the Caledonian (still the 'Caley' to many locals). Princes Street, with shops on the north side and the castle and the Old Town on the south, is one of the world's great streets, partly known for the upmarket shops that brought people into the city centre and, of course, for the views. Most of the great shops have gone, and today Princes Street offers the same selection of shops as many high streets, but it is still an important focal point. There is one tramstop, Princes Street, an island stop, sitting just west of the junction with The Mound, the street that climbs up to the Old Town. Edinburgh's last first-generation trams slowly descended The Mound on Friday, 16 November 1956, turning into Princes Street and following a similar route to the new trams towards their final destination, Shrubhill.

Edinburgh grew up in what is now known as the Old Town, with housing and shops crowded around the High Street, and from the tram you can glimpse on the right the crown spire of St Giles' Cathedral, the High Kirk of Edinburgh, and, at the top of The Mound, looking over to the New Town, is the fine 19th-century Bank of Scotland Headquarters. Also prominent is the University of Edinburgh's New College, and to its right sits the attractive clutch of private apartment buildings, Ramsay Garden, nestling beside the Castle Esplanade – and potentially noisy when the annual Royal Edinburgh Military Tattoo is held on the esplanade each August. Between Princes Street and the Old Town, at a lower level, are Princes Street Gardens, with the main railway route west nestling under the castle rock.

The driver's view as trams pass in Princes Street in June 2014, surrounded by buses and a taxi.

ABOVE: Viewed from a high-level path in West Princes Street Gardens in August 2014, a tram heads west along Princes Street, passing the Royal Scots Greys statue.

RIGHT: Princes Street at the Frederick Street junction in March 2017 and 251 wears Tramspotting advertising in the Edinburgh Trams pink, promoting the trams.

Day One of the new Edinburgh trams in May 2014 and crowds flock on to the island platform at the Princes Street stop, at last able to ride on the trams they had been waiting for.

ABOVE: The popular Princes Street island tramstop sits between eastbound and westbound traffic lanes that are restricted to buses and taxis for much of the day. This is a February 2017 shot, with the passenger information on the left showing that it is 1521hrs, and the tram for the Airport has just arrived, with another due in six minutes.

BELOW LEFT: May 2014, just weeks before the trams started carrying passengers, and 255 sits at the Princes Street traffic lights at the Hanover Street/Mound junction. Since then, two major stores in that block, British Home Stores and Jenners, have stopped trading.

BELOW RIGHT: Christmas shoppers in Princes Street in December 2018 as a tram passes the Scott Monument.

ABOVE: The Balmoral Hotel, built as the North British Station Hotel in 1902, dominates the east end of Princes Street. Tram 252 is airport-bound, under a threatening sky in April 2016.

RIGHT: July 2014 and 274 has just turned right from South St Andrew Street on to Princes Street, with the Balmoral Hotel clock showing the time – albeit traditionally two minutes fast for train travellers hurrying to Waverley Station in the valley below.

Back on Princes Street, and our tram passes the amazing 200ft-high Victorian Gothic Scott Monument inaugurated in 1846 to remember the Edinburgh-born writer Sir Walter Scott, and just beyond, sitting in the valley between the city's Old and New Towns is Edinburgh's main railway station, Waverley, named after Sir Walter Scott's Waverley novels. Our tram then takes a sharp left to St Andrew Square, once home to many of the financial institutions that played an important role in the city's growth. The St Andrew Square tramstop is adjacent to the public gardens in the middle of the square, dominated by the 150ft-high Melville Monument, remembering Henry Dundas, the first Viscount Melville, who in recent years has become notorious as a politician who delayed the abolition of the slave trade. Building Edinburgh's New Town started in St Andrew Square in 1772 for wealthier people who wanted to escape the cramped and squalid conditions of the Old Town, built around the High Street, moving to new housing to the north of the city centre.

ABOVE: This February 2016 photo illustrates the full 42.8m (140.42ft) length of the Edinburgh trams, and the variety of architectural styles in the Old Town in the background.

LEFT: The Scots describe a dull, wet, dreary, cold day like this as 'dreich'. Passengers brave the elements in October 2022 to catch a tram to the Airport at the St Andrew Square stop. At this time, trams from the Airport were terminating here because of tramworks in York Place and Picardy Place.

Tram 267 turns from North St Andrew Street into York Place in May 2017, passing the impressive red sandstone Gothic revival bulk of the 1889 Scottish National Portrait Gallery as the city slopes away towards the Firth of Forth.

ABOVE LEFT: Seen from a passing bus, 269 slows as it reaches its terminus at York Place in June 2016. The buildings that line York Place mostly date from the 18th century; the artist Henry Raeburn had his studio at number 32, indicated by a rendition of a palette on the outside wall.

ABOVE RIGHT: Tram 277 proceeds along York Place in July 2021. The York Place stop was permanently closed in 2022, although trams terminating at St Andrew Square continued to York Place to use the crossover there. Cycle lanes have been installed here in recent years, as in many other parts of Edinburgh.

At times during the construction of the line that now continues to Newhaven, St Andrew Square was the terminus for the route from the Airport. The main terminus was originally at York Place, a short distance further east, but the single-platform York Place stop had a relatively short life and the platform was dismantled in 2022 and the new Picardy Place stop was built on the other side of a busy road junction. The trams terminating at St Andrew Square still had to go to York Place with its trailing crossover to start their return journeys.

The York Place concrete still looks very new as 269, still with its bright red stripe, heads west on the first stage of its journey in June 2014.

ABOVE LEFT: The original eastern terminus of Line 1 was at York Place, where passengers crowd the platform for their first ride on the new trams on 1 June 2014, the second day of operation.

ABOVE RIGHT: Dusk at the York Place stop in November 2014 as the driver of 272 awaits his departure time for the Airport.

A general view of the Picardy Place tramstop in March 2024; the all-green Ovo tram is about to start its long descent down Leith Walk towards the Firth of Forth, and the World of Illusions tram is heading to the Airport. This centre of this triangular road junction has been landscaped and contains a statue of Sherlock Holmes.

Proceeding from the island platform at St Andrew Square stop, our tram passes the Scottish National Portrait Gallery on the left and Edinburgh Bus Station on the right, before turning into York Place, a street of fine 18th-century buildings. For nine years, York Place was as far as the budget could stretch for the new trams, but from 7 June 2023, the tram route carried passengers east then north towards Leith and Newhaven for the first time. The island platform at Picardy Place is convenient for the large St James Quarter shopping and hotel complex, the Playhouse cinema, St Mary's Catholic Cathedral, the Omni Centre with cinemas and restaurants, as well as a multitude of smaller restaurants and bars. And there are glimpses of Calton Hill before our tram turns left for its long descent of Leith Walk towards the Firth of Forth. This street boasts a wide variety of shops, cafes, restaurants and bars, as well as some historical links with local transport. The first is Annandale Street, leading off to the left, where one of Lothian Buses' garages is housed in a building dating back more than a century; it first functioned as a bus garage in 1926 and now also houses Lothian's head office. As Leith Walk continues north, our tram passes a new housing development built on the site of the massive Shrubhill complex, which was used for the maintenance of Edinburgh's trams and buses for over a century, and the place where the majority of Edinburgh's first-generation electric trams were built. Although the area is named The Engine Yard, the second phase, which incorporates buildings from the original transport complex, is appropriately named The Tram Sheds.

RIGHT: The tramstop at Picardy Place replaced the York Place stop when the through service to Newhaven started on 7 June 2023. The stop forms one side of a large triangular one-way traffic island, and is now home to this statue of Sherlock Holmes, the detective created by Sir Arthur Conan Doyle, who was born close to this spot in 1859; it is a rare statue of a fictional character.

BELOW: Tram 276 sits at the Picardy Place stop in in March 2024, heading for the Airport, when it will pass St Paul's and St George's Church, opened in 1818.

This Airport-bound tram passes through Elm Row in July 2023 with Leith Walk stretching in the left background towards Leith and Newhaven. It is promoting the annual Edinburgh International Festival, one of several festivals that take place in the city each August.

The first of two island-platform tramstops in Leith Walk is at McDonald Road, immediately opposite the long-established Harburn Hobbies model shop, a popular destination for local enthusiasts. A shop window sign, in the style of the famous British Railways totem logo, announces it as Harburn Halt.

At the Pilrig Street junction, we cross what was until 1920 the boundary of the two separate burghs of Edinburgh and Leith, scene of what was known then as the Pilrig Muddle. In the late 19th century, Edinburgh had decided to replace its horse-drawn trams with cable cars, which were attached to constantly-moving cables under the ground, between the tram tracks; Leith, like the great majority of towns and cities at the time, opted for electric trams with overhead wires. So, passengers wanting to proceed beyond Pilrig in both

The first Leith Walk tramstop is at McDonald Road adjacent to Harburn Hobbies, a long-established Leith Walk business, selling model railways, diecast buses and transport books. In this March 2024 view, note the Harburn Halt signs in the style of British Rail Scottish Region totems.

Leaving McDonald Road, Newhaven-bound trams cross what was until 1920 the boundary between the separate burghs of Edinburgh and Leith. In this March 2024 view, the front part of 265 is now in Leith with the rear part still in Edinburgh.

directions had to change trams – a short walk over the boundary, no problem on a fine day but less fun on a cold, wet day. Local train services benefited in the short term, until Leith was reluctantly absorbed into Edinburgh in 1920, and passengers flocked on to the new direct electric trams.

Just north of Pilrig is Iona Street, displaying two large cable-winding wheels, rescued during the recent tramworks, as a reminder of past trams – though not the trams that passed the end of Iona Street, which is just in what was Leith, which never had cable trams. The other tramstop in Leith Walk is Balfour Street, another island platform with an adjacent trailing crossover. Another reminder of the trams is further down Leith Walk, the office block on the right that sat at the entrance to Leith tram depot, later an Edinburgh Corporation bus garage. All traces of the depot/garage have gone, but the office block survives.

The Balfour Street tramstop serves the lower part of Leith Walk. Tram 259 is bound for Newhaven in March 2024.

In Iona Street, just in pre-1920 Leith, are two cable-winding wheels, mounted as a reminder of the cable trams that used to terminate a few yards away on the Edinburgh side of the boundary. They were discovered in August 2021 during the construction of the tramway down Leith Walk.

LEFT: Leaving the Balfour Street stop, trams pass the recently renovated art deco building, The Red Sandstone. The Newhaven Trams car, 258, in July 2023.

BELOW: On the east side of Leith Walk is the 1930s admin block, all that remains of Leith tram depot, seen here in March 2024.

Enjoy the Journey

The Foot of Leith Walk is still very much the heart of Leith, and our tram crosses the busy road junction into a tram-only section of Constitution Street and the Foot of the Walk two-platform tramstop, the only stop that is completely open to the elements. Our tram continues down Constitution Street, along one of the routes followed by Edinburgh's first-generation trams until 1956, passing Leith Police Station, remembered by many for the tongue-twister 'The Leith Police dismisseth us'. Passing popular cafes on the left, our tram reaches The Shore tramstop. The first-generation trams turned left after this point into the broad expanse of Bernard Street, a collection of fine buildings that were once home to the shipping and associated companies reflecting Leith's importance as an international port.

RIGHT: Tram 254 drifts down Leith Walk to the Foot of the Walk tramstop in June 2023.

BELOW: The Foot of Leith Walk is very much the heart of Leith; 268 crosses the busy junction towards the tram-only section of Constitution Street in June 2023, where the Foot of the Walk stop is situated. Although the tramboard suggests it is Airport-bound, it is heading towards Newhaven.

The Foot of the Walk stop is squeezed into the south end of Constitution Street, and is the only stop with no shelter for passengers. Trams 265 and 264 meet at the stop in June 2023.

LEFT: Tram 254 has just left the stop at The Shore, heading to the Airport in August 2023.

BELOW: In August 2023, tram 262 leaves the tramstop at The Shore and crosses busy Bernard Street towards Newhaven.

A statue to Robert Burns, Scotland's national bard, dominates the junction of Constitution Street and Bernard Street; tram 252 passes it in March 2024.

Our tram continues towards the former Dock Gates into an area that was once a part of Leith's extensive docklands, now private housing around the Port of Leith stop, and continuing west, there are good views across the docks. As Leith is still a working port – the largest deepwater port in Scotland – it is regularly visited by merchant ships, naval vessels and cruise liners.

Tram 276 skirts Leith Docks on its way to Newhaven.

ABOVE: Tram 264 has just passed the *Fingal* floating hotel, moored in Alexandra Dock in Leith, heading for the Airport in August 2023. The historic dock building on the right on Prince of Wales Dock, is now the head office of Forth Ports Ltd, with ports throughout the UK.

MIDDLE: There are glimpses of Leith Docks on the stretch between the Port of Leith and Ocean Terminal stops. This is Airport-bound 252 in June 2023. The next photo was taken from the black Port of Leith Distillery to the right of the tram.

LEFT: In February 2024, a tram crosses the bridge on Ocean Drive that sits alongside the historic Victoria Swing Bridge.

Enjoy the Journey

Passing the *Fingal*, a luxury floating hotel that in an earlier life was a lighthouse tender vessel, our tram crosses the Water of Leith, passing a former swing bridge. The view then opens on the left to Victoria Quay, the massive Scottish government office built on redeveloped dockland, which helped regenerate this part of Leith, attracting new housing, bars and restaurants. Ahead is the Ocean Terminal shopping, cinema and restaurant complex, and our tram heads left to the Ocean Terminal tramstop, in an area that is also terminus for some Lothian Buses routes. Our tram then heads right towards its Newhaven terminus, passing more of the dock area, and passengers looking back or travelling on rearward-facing seats, will catch a glimpse of the former Royal Yacht *Britannia*, moored alongside Ocean Terminal since 1998 and a hugely popular visitor attraction.

The Newhaven two-platform terminus is just short of a busy road junction and beyond this is Newhaven Harbour, with cafes and restaurants. In time the tramway could continue east past the harbour, to meet a future Roseburn–Granton line further along the coast.

RIGHT: Tram 275 has left the Ocean Terminal stop in December 2023 on its journey to the Airport. Much new housing is being built in this area, which sits on reclaimed land.

BELOW: There is a crossover at Ocean Terminal for short-working trams and 275 uses it to start its next trip to the Airport in December 2023.

In June 2023, tram 269 approaches the Ocean Terminal stop, heading for Newhaven rather than the destination shown on the tramboard. The tram carries advertising promoting Lothian Buses' open-top tours.

With Ocean Terminal in the background on the right and the former Royal Yacht *Britannia* on the left, 254 climbs towards the terminus at Newhaven in September 2023.

ABOVE: Tram 272 is dwarfed by the Oceania Cruises MS *Nautica,* berthed in Leith in August 2024.

RIGHT: Signs a-plenty and a double crossover, looking towards the Newhaven terminus. Tram 259 prepares to depart for the Airport in February 2024.

Tram 267 uses the crossover at the start of its journey in June 2023.

Passengers leave 262 at Newhaven in June 2023 while another tram departs for the Airport. Both platforms are used for arrivals and departures at Newhaven, as at the Airport.

Tram 261 at Newhaven terminus in September 2024 at what was the end of the line at the time. Future plans include extending the tramway west from this point to connect with a new line linking Granton and Haymarket.

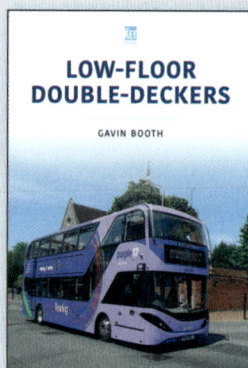

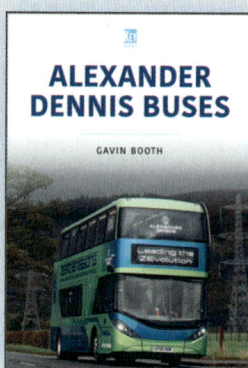

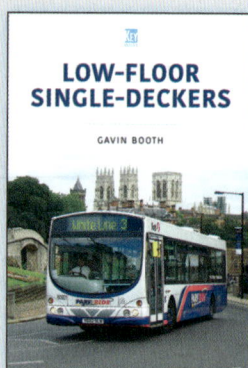

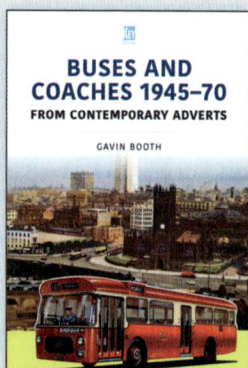

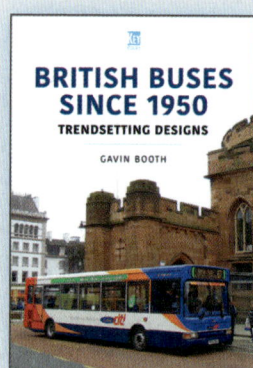